Junior praise

PRAYERS
AND
READINGS

Junior praise

PRAYERS
AND
READINGS

Rebecca Harris

Marshall Pickering

Marshall Morgan and Scott
Marshall Pickering
3 Beggarwood Lane, Basingstoke, Hants RG23 7LP, UK

First published in 1986 by
Marshall Morgan and Scott Publications Ltd
Part of the Marshall Pickering Holdings Group
A subsidiary of the Zondervan Corporation

Reprinted 2nd Impression 1988

British Library CIP Data
Junior praise prayers and readings.
   1. Schools—Great Britain—Prayers
   2. Schools—Great Britain—Exercises
and recreations
   I. Horrobin, Peter   II. Leavers, Greg
   377'.1   BV283.S3

   ISBN 0-551-01396-6

Text Set in Linotron Palatino (Headings Rockwell) by
Input Typesetting Ltd, London
Printed in Great Britain by
The Guernsey Press Co. Ltd., Guernsey, Channel Islands.

Contents

Introduction and Acknowledgements   vii
1. Advent   1
2. Christmas   4
3. Lent   8
4. Palm Sunday   11
5. Easter and Holy Week   13
6. Ascension   21
7. Pentecost (Whitsun)   23
8. Harvest   26
9. God the Father   30
10. Jesus   40
11. The Holy Spirit   53
12. The Trinity   57
13. Bible Stories   59
14. The Bible and Scripture   74
15. Blessings and the Doxology   79
16. Christian Living   82
17. Church   97
18. Commitment   101
19. Confession   107
20. Friends and Family   114
21. God in Creation   121
22. Guidance   127
23. Health and Healing   133
24. Missions   138
25. Morning and Evening   145
26. Praise and Thanksgiving   151
27. Prayers and Praying   167
28. Service and Giving   172
29. Times of Sadness   177
30. Work and Play   181

Introduction and Acknowledgements

These prayers and Bible readings have been written and compiled to be used alongside the young people's song book, *Junior Praise*.

The readings chosen to accompany each song have been taken from every part of the Bible, both Old and New Testament, and include stories and teaching passages. It is hoped that in this way young people will become familiar with the message of the Bible through the year and begin to understand its significance and relevance in today's world.

The prayers have been compiled under various section headings, as have the hymns and songs, to enable those leading worship to find material especially suited to particular occasions. They have been written specifically with children and young people in mind, the aim being to express as prayers the thoughts and feelings of young people as they seek to live out the Christian life, and to draw them into a closer relationship with the Lord Jesus.

I would particularly like to ackowledge the contribution of Gordon Bailey, whose prayers for teenagers from his book, *I want to tell you how I feel, God* (Lion Publishers), have been included with his kind permission.

I am also grateful to many friends for their involvement and help in both the preparation and compilation of this book, especially Hilary Price, a school teacher, who has written several of the prayers, and also my fiancé, Andrew Silver, who has both contributed material and been a tremendous encouragement to me in the preparation of the book.

Rebecca Harris
August 1986

1 Advent

Hark the glad
sound   68

Matthew chapter 17 verses 14–21
Matthew chapter 21 verses 1–11

How lovely on the
mountains   84

Isaiah chapter 59 verses 1–9,
chapter 60 verses 1–3
Isaiah chapter 45 verses 17–24
Isaiah chapter 52 verses 7–10

Jesus how lovely you
are   133

Revelation chapter 22 verses 1–17
Luke chapter 24 verses 1–12
Revelation chapter 19 verses 1–9

O come O come,
Emmanuel   177

Isaiah chapter 9 verses 6, 7
Malachi chapter 4 verses 1–4
Isaiah chapter 59 verses 16–21,
chapter 60 verses 1–5

O when the
saints   195

Revelation chapter 4 verses 1–11
Revelation chapter 20 verses
11–15, chapter 21 verses 1–5
Revelation chapter 19 verses 1–9
Philippians chapter 2 verses 5–11

On Jordan's bank the
Baptist's cry   186

Matthew chapter 3 verses 1–17
John chapter 1 verses 6–8, 15–37

Our eyes have seen the
glory   191

See Ascension

Prayers for Advent

Dear God, The Bible tells us that at the end of the Old Testament when you had brought the Israelites back to Israel and they had built the temple again in Jerusalem, there was a gap of four hundred years when nothing special happened in their lives, and then Jesus came. Just as the Israelites must have waited all those years for Jesus, we are waiting and looking forward to Christmas.

Please make this Christmas as special a time to us this year as it was when Jesus was born and help us to enjoy these next weeks as we prepare to celebrate His birthday.

In Jesus' Name, Amen.

Dear Lord, I can't wait for Christmas. There are only four weeks left now and there's still lots to get ready, cards to send to people, presents to choose and probably parties to go to. As we enjoy all these things, please help us to remember the real story of Christmas and to get ready to celebrate Jesus' birthday. We pray for all those people who won't be able to have presents and fun at Christmas because they don't have any money. Please look after them and help them and us to understand that those aren't the things that will give us a happy Christmas; it's more important that we know you and love you.

In Jesus' Name, Amen.

Dear Lord Jesus, John the Baptist must have been a very special person to know that you had come into the world to save people from their sins and bring them back to God. Even before He was born He was filled with Your Holy Spirit and prepared to be a messenger to tell others about you. We want to be messengers like Him; filled with your Holy Spirit and prepared to tell others that you are alive and waiting to come into their lives. Please use us as you used Him, in such a special way.

In your Name, Amen.

Dear Lord Jesus, When John the Baptist started to preach and tell others that God's Son had come to earth and was very close to them, they must have been very excited, but also very aware of how many things they needed to put right in their lives before they met Him. In this Advent time, as we wait for Christmas and the celebration of your coming into the world, please help us to put things right in our lives that we know are wrong. Thank you that as John and his friends were able to meet with you on the banks of the river Jordan, we can meet you today in our hearts. Thank you for your presence with us this morning, may we be aware of you in all that we do throughout the day.

In your Name, Amen.

2   Christmas

As with gladness men of old   9

Matthew chapter 2 verses 1–12
Luke chapter 2 verses 1–7

Angels from the realms of glory   10

Luke chapter 2 verses 8–20

Away in a manger   12

Luke chapter 2 verses 4–7

Come and praise the Lord our King   34

Luke chapter 2 verses 8–14
Matthew chapter 1 verses 18–25
Luke chapter 1 verses 26–33

Ding dong! Merrily on high   38

Luke chapter 2 verses 8–14
Luke chapter 1 verses 46–56

Glory to God in the highest   51

Luke chapter 2 verses 8–14
Revelation chapter 19 verses 11–16

Hark! The herald angels sing   69

Luke chapter 2 verses 8–14
John chapter 1 verses 1–14
Malachi chapter 4 verses 1–4

Infant holy, Infant lowly   110

Luke chapter 2 verses 1–20
Luke chapter 2 verses 21–35

It came upon the midnight clear   116

Luke chapter 2 verses 8–14
Luke chapter 2 verses 21–35

Jesus Christ the Lord is born   131

Luke chapter 2 verses 15–20
Matthew chapter 2 verses 13–23

Mary had a little baby   164

Matthew chapter 1 verses 18–25
Luke chapter 1 verses 26–56

O come all you faithful   176

John chapter 1 verses 1–14
Luke chapter 2 verses 8–20

O little town of Bethlehem   182

Micah chapter 5 verses 1–5
Matthew chapter 2 verses 1–12

Once in royal David's city   185

Matthew chapter 2 verses 1–12
Luke chapter 2 verses 1–7

See amid the winter's snow   213

Isaiah chapter 9 verses 6–7
Luke chapter 2 verses 1–7
John chapter 1 verses 1–14

See Him lying on a bed of straw   214

Luke chapter 2 verses 4–20
Luke chapter 1 verses 46–56

Silent night   219

Luke chapter 2 verses 1–20
Luke chapter 2 verses 25–35

The first Nowell   238

Luke chapter 2 verses 8–20

The Virgin Mary had a baby boy   251

Luke chapter 1 verses 26–38
Luke chapter 2 verses 46–56
Matthew chapter 2 verses 1–12

Unto us a boy is born   263

Isaiah chapter 9 verses 6–7
Micah chapter 5 verses 1–5
Luke chapter 2 verses 1–7

We three Kings   271

Matthew chapter 2 verses 1–12
Micah chapter 5 verses 1–5

While shepherds watched their flocks by night   285

Luke chapter 2 verses 8–20

Prayers for Christmas

Dear Heavenly Father, This is the time of year when we are all wanting to give gifts to the people we love. In some small way we want to give our parents, our brothers, our sisters, and all our relations something costly because we love them. Help us to realise this Christmas that you sent your one and only Son as a gift of love to each one of us in order that we might see in Him the way to live. Help us also to realise that it cost you everything to send Jesus, because He had to die so that we can be made your friends again.

Thank you God, Amen.

Dear God, Mary must have been very special to you as you chose her to give birth to your son. Thank you that it was a miracle because you were up in heaven yet you placed your seed in Mary who was down here on earth. Thank you also for Joseph who stayed with Mary as she gave birth to your son. Help us, Lord God, to understand that just as you placed your seed in Mary you can place your Spirit in us. Thank you that just like her we are special to you and Jesus can live in each one of us.

Thank you Lord, Amen.

Heavenly Father, How wonderful it is to think back to the night when your son was born on earth. He was a king from all the glory of heaven, yet became a tiny baby in a dirty manger. We can imagine there was a hush in heaven as He was born and then when His first cries were heard, no doubt all the people broke out into song!

Thank you He was born to die for us. Thank you that He loved us from that first moment and came to bring us back to you. He wasn't just an ordinary baby, He came to save us from our sins. Help us to accept Him and love Him in return.

In His Precious Name, Amen.

Lord, Christmas is a great time of year. We have holidays and parties, lots of food and lots of presents. Sometimes I wonder why you were born in a stable full of hay when you could have been born in a palace. Help me to remember that when I eat my food and receive my presents this Christmas, there are many people who are living in barns and stables because they have no homes to go to. Show me how to help to make their Christmas a special one.

In your Name, Amen.

Lord Jesus, We want to bow down before you in adoration just as the wise men knelt before you in a stable in Bethlehem two thousand years ago. Our lives are yours Lord, we give them to you to do with them what you want. Lord, take them as an expression of our love for you.

In your precious Name, Amen.

Dear Lord Jesus, It must have been an amazing sight to see the hosts of angels singing praises to you. The day that you were born, heaven recognised that you were the Messiah. It is so sad that people on earth today reject you as the Messiah. Help us this Christmas to accept you and not reject you, and help us to give you all the praise that you deserve.

Amen.

Father, Thank you for sending your son Jesus to earth. His birthplace was humble, yet shepherds and wise men came to see and adore Him. He was brought up as an ordinary child – yet, there was a difference about His life. He came to earth for a purpose and that was to save men and to allow them to have a personal relationship with you. Through His death we can now live a life full of riches – a life as you intended.

Jesus was the prince of glory and still is today. Let us give Him his rightful place in our lives.

In His Name, Amen.

Dear Lord, Thank you for Christmastime. Thank you for the presents we receive and for the festivities and celebrations. Help us not to get caught up in the fun side of Christmas and forget what Christmas is all about. The wise men gave gifts of gold, frankinscence and myrrh. Help us this year to give you our thanks as a gift for coming into this world.

Amen.

3　Lent

Dear Lord and Father of mankind　37

Romans chapter 12 verses 1–8
Matthew chapter 4 verses 18–22
Genesis chapter 27 verses 1–46

Father, hear the prayer we offer　41

Luke chapter 22 verses 39–46
Mark chapter 1 verses 35–39
Genesis chapter 39 verses 1–23

Father lead me day by day　43

Luke chapter 4 verses 1–13
Mark chapter 1 verses 9–13
Exodus chapter 14 verses 1–31

I'm feeding on the living bread　104

John chapter 4 verses 1–15
John chapter 6 verses 25–59
Exodus chapter 16 verses 1–36

Let us praise God together　152

John chapter 17 verses 1–5
2 Timothy verses 1–10

Prayers for Lent

SHROVE TUESDAY

Dear God, Today we are going to have pancakes to eat; I like pancakes, but what have they got to do with you? Pancakes are made with egg and milk which is very nourishing and good for us. Tomorrow we remember that Jesus went away into the wilderness and didn't eat anything for forty days and forty nights, so I suppose eating pancakes reminds us of the food that Jesus went without while He was in the wilderness. Thank you that we never have to go without food because you always give us as much as we need. Many people won't have anything to eat today, so please help us to appreciate all the food that we have.

In Jesus' Name, Amen.

ASH WEDNESDAY

Dear Heavenly Father, Thank you that we have a special day to remind us of the time that Jesus went away into the wilderness for forty days and nights all alone, and with nothing to eat. Please help us to use the time between today and Easter to remember the difficult things that Jesus did to show that He loves us, and to make it possible for us to be your friend. Thank you that He never turned away from hardship, but but even allowed himself to be put to death for our sakes. Thank you for your love.

Amen.

Dear Lord Jesus, It must have been a very lonely time for you when you went away into the wilderness for forty days; and you didn't eat anything all that time. I even get hungry if I miss *one* meal, so you must have been almost starving. And then Satan came and tempted you to turn the stones into bread so you could eat; I don't think that I could have refused if it had been me. Please help me to say 'no' when I am offered wrong things, and help me to read the Bible to find out what is pleasing to you and what you won't want in our lives. Help me to be like you when I am tempted and to use your power to resist.

In your Name. Amen.

Dear Lord Jesus, When you were all alone in the wilderness and hungry and weak, Satan came to tempt you with food to satisfy your body; nations and wealth to satisfy your ambition and spiritual power to satisfy your pride, but you refused and chose instead to be obedient to God, your Father. Thank you for your example of obedience, and please teach me to do the things that are right rather than going my own way to satisfy myself.

In your Name, Amen.

Dear Heavenly Father, Just as this time of Lent prepares us for Easter, so Jesus' time in the wilderness was preparing Him for His crucifixtion by testing His obedience to you and His willingness to do what you wanted. Thank you that because He was perfect in His obedience He was able to go

to the cross and die as a sacrifice for us. Thank you that Jesus was willing to obey so that I could be set free from my sins.
In His precious Name, Amen.

4 Palm Sunday

Children of
  Jerusalem   24

Psalm 149
Matthew chapter 19 verses 13–15

Ride on, ride on in
  majesty   209

Mark chapter 11 verses 1–11
Luke chapter 19 verses 28–44

We have a king who
  rides on a
  donkey   264

Matthew chapter 21 verses 1–11
Luke chapter 19 verses 28–44

Prayers for Palm Sunday

Lord Jesus, Everyone lined the roads to cheer and wave palm branches when you rode into Jerusalem, because they thought you had come as king to overthrow those who ruled over them. But you didn't ride into the city on a horse as a great king going to battle, but on a donkey, knowing that you were riding to your death. You didn't come to be king of a country, but king of the whole universe and before you could take the throne you had to buy your kingdom back for yourself through your death.

Thank you that today you reign in heaven and we can praise you as our king. Praise you king Jesus.

Amen.

A man gave you his donkey Lord Jesus, for you to ride into Jerusalem. What a special honour for him to give you something that you could use. Please show me if there is anything I have that you could use, even if it means giving something special to someone else who doesn't have as much as I have. Please take my life and use it for yourself.

I ask this for your sake, Amen.

Lord Jesus, Not many people really understood what was happening when you came to Jerusalem, they didn't realise that you had come knowing you would be put to death.

There are a lot of people today who don't understand why you came to earth and what you did when you died for us. It's sad that not many people know that you came to bring us new life. We pray that you will help us to explain to all our friends what you have done and that they will understand and come to you for new life.

We ask this in your Name, Amen.

5   Easter and Holy Week

Alleluia, Alleluia, give thanks to the risen Lord   3

Romans chapter 6 verses 3–10
Matthew chapter 28 verses 1–10

Barabbas was a bad man   18

Matthew chapter 27 verses 11–26
Luke chapter 23 verses 13–25

God sent His Son   58

Luke chapter 24 verses 1–49
Luke chapter 19 verses 1–10
John chapter 14 verses 15–26

God's not dead   60

Ephesians chapter 3 verses 14–19
Luke chapter 24 verses 1–12

He is Lord   75

Acts chapter 2 verses 34–36
Philippians chapter 2 verses 5–11
1 Corinthians chapter 15 verses 25–27

He paid a debt   77

Romans chapter 5 verses 1–8
Ephesians chapter 2 verses 1–10

I met you at the cross   103

John chapter 19 verses 25–30
Luke chapter 23 verses 33–43

I serve a risen Saviour   113

Matthew chapter 28 verses 1–9
John chapter 11 verses 1–27
Romans chapter 5 verses 1–10
Hebrews chapter 5 verses 5a–8

It be a thing most wonderful   117

Romans chapter 5 verses 1–11
John chapter 3 verses 14–18
John chapter 14 verses 15–21

I will sing the wondrous story   127

Luke chapter 15 verses 1–7
John chapter 5 verses 19–30
John chapter 20 verses 24–31

Jesus Christ is alive today 129

I Corinthians chapter 15 verses 12–26
Colossians chapter 1 verses 9–19
Ephesians chapter 3 verses 14–19

Jesus Christ is risen today 130

Luke chapter 24 verses 1–12
Hebrews chapter 11 verses 1–6
Romans chapter 5 verses 1–11

Jesus died for all the children 132

John chapter 3 verses 14–17
Mark chapter 10 verses 13–16

Jesus is Lord! 137

Colossians chapter 1 verses 9–20
Romans chapter 1 verses 18–20
Psalm 19

Led like a lamb 151

Luke chapter 22 verses 39–65
Luke chapter 22 verse 66, chapter 23 verse 25
Matthew chapter 28 verses 1–10
Luke chapter 24 verses 13–32
Genesis chapter 22 verses 1–17

Live, live, live 153

Isaiah chapter 53
John chapter 9 verses 1–25
Acts chapter 17 verses 22–28

Low in the grave He lay 159

Matthew chapter 27 verse 57, chapter 28 verse 10
Luke chapter 23 verse 50, chapter 24 verse 12
Acts chapter 2 verses 14, 22–36

On the love that drew salvation's plan 181

John chapter 3 verses 14–17
Ephesians chapter 2 verses 1–22
1 Peter chapter 1 verses 18–21

On Calvary's tree He died for me 183

Luke chapter 23 verses 26–46
John chapter 8 verses 31–36
Genesis chapter 22 verses 1–17
Exodus chapter 12 verses 1–13

One day when heaven was filled with His praises 187

Isaiah chapter 53 verses 1–9
Matthew chapter 27 verses 32–56
Luke chapter 24 verses 1–12

Saviour of the world 216

Luke chapter 22 verses 39–53
Luke chapter 23 verses 33–49

There is a green hill far away 245

John chapter 19 verses 16–30
Luke chapter 23 verses 33–49
Hebrews chapter 10 verses 1–17
Ephesians chapter 2 verses 1–10

This joyful Eastertide 256

1 Corinthians chapter 15 verses 1–20
1 Corinthians chapter 15 verses 51–57
Matthew chapter 28 verses 1–10

Were you there when they crucified my Lord 269

Luke chapter 23 verses 26–49
Matthew chapter 28 verses 1–10
Matthew chapter 27 verses 27–56

What a wonderful Saviour is Jesus 274

Philippians chapter 2 verses 1–11
1 Thessalonians chapter 4 verses 13–18

When I survey the wondrous cross 277

Psalm 22
Matthew chapter 27 verses 27–50
Luke chapter 23

Yours be the glory 299

Matthew chapter 28 verses 1–10
1 Corinthians chapter 15 verses 1–20
Romans chapter 5 verses 1–11

Prayers for Easter and Holy Week

Heavenly Father, It's hard for us to understand why you sent your Son Jesus to die on the cross. Why did He have to pay for all the wrong we have done when He had never done anything but good? How could you leave Him when He was suffering on the cross so that He cried out, 'My God, My God, Why have you forsaken me?' It must have been the hardest thing to do; to watch your only son being put to death knowing that you had the power to stop it, but knowing that He must go through it if death and sin were to be overcome.

Father, we are amazed by your love that allowed this to happen for our sakes; so we could be forgiven and receive your new life. Please help us to believe and trust in Jesus so that by His death, we might have life.

Amen.

Lord God, All through the Old Testament people came to the temple to sacrifice animals as a symbol that their sins could be forgiven. Every time they did something wrong they would have to come again with another animal.

We praise you and thank you that when Jesus came He was the 'Lamb of God', sent to be a sacrifice for all our sins. Because He died we no longer have to make sacrifices for our sin. As we trust in Him, our sins are forgiven and we can know peace with you.

Thank you God for sending Jesus, Amen.

Lord Jesus, Even before the creation of this world you knew that one day you would come to earth to die, taking upon yourself the punishment that men deserved for turning away from God and living sinful lives. Even as you and your Father created men and gave them life, you knew that those same men would turn against you and put you to death. As you sat around the table sharing a meal of friendship with your disciples you knew that even then one of them was planning to betray you.

Throughout history you have chosen to love us, to give yourself for us and to make us your friends, and yet men have chosen to despise and reject you and the life you came to give them.

Forgive us, Lord Jesus, for the times we have rejected your love and turned away from you. Thank you that you died for us even though we live such ungrateful lives. Help us to show you our thanks by accepting your love and friendship, and by living our lives for your glory.

We ask this in your Name, Amen.

Jesus, Thank you that you are Lord of the whole earth. Thank you that you left heaven and came to earth to die on a cross to take away our sin. It must have been so hard to be a king and to give up everything – even your life. Thank you that the story didn't stop there, but you rose from the dead and are alive today. This means that now you want to live as Lord in each person's life. The Bible says one day we'll all bow before you and call you Lord. Help us to have the courage to do that today and not put it off.

In your Name, Amen.

Lord Jesus, We thank you so much for your love to us. We know that it cost you a lot to show us just how much you love us: you left your home in heaven and came down to live with men on earth. All through your life you loved people. You healed the sick, you taught people about God and His love for them. But even though you loved people so much, they turned against you and put you to death because they hated you. And as you were dying on the cross you asked God to forgive those people. We don't understand how you can love people in that way, but we thank you that you allowed yourself to be put to death so that each one of us can be forgiven for all the things that we have done wrong and can know you as our Saviour and friend.

In your Name we pray, Amen.

Lord Jesus, You say in the Bible, 'greater love has no man than he lay down his life for his brother'. You laid down your life for us so that we could be forgiven for all that we have done wrong and could become your friends. Thank you for showing us such a great love.

In your Name, Amen.

Dear Lord Jesus, What a sad time it must have been for your disciples and friends when you died on the cross. They thought you had come to rule as king but instead you were arrested, beaten and crucified by your enemies. For them it was as if you were completely defeated, but you knew that by dying and then being raised from death, you would in fact defeat the greatest enemy of all men: death.

How wonderful for the disciples when they discovered that you were alive again, and how wonderful for us to know that you are alive and reigning in heaven as king. Thank you for your victory over death.

In your Name, Amen.

Dear Lord Jesus, Even our best friends can hurt us sometimes, without meaning to, and it makes us very sad. But one of your twelve disciples who had spent so much time with you and gone around as your friend, betrayed you to your enemies, knowing that it would lead to your death. And then all the other disciples left you one by one, and Peter even denied that he ever knew you. So you had to face your trial and death all alone: just you against all those people who hated you. It makes me hurt inside to think how lonely you must have been. Thank you that you went through that loneliness for my sake – please help me to be a true friend to you and to others.

In your Name, Amen.

Oh God, Thank you for the marvellous fact that Jesus is alive today. Thank you that He isn't just someone from history nearly 2,000 years ago who was killed and buried and that was the end of it. Thank you that Jesus rose from the dead and wants to live in each of us. Not only to forgive us for our sins but to save us from our sins day by day. That's why we can call Him Saviour. He can come into our lives and turn them upside down. There is no-one like Jesus. No-one has ever matched his personality and power and no-one ever will. Thank you God that He is alive – giving us His personality and His power – when we let Him.

In His Name, Amen.

Lord Jesus, Thank you that you left heaven to come to earth for us. Thank you that you loved us so much that you chose to come and die for us so that we might be forgiven. We're so glad that you did not stay dead and that we can know you as our friend because you are alive today.

In your Name, Amen.

Lord Jesus, When Thomas the disciple doubted that you were alive again, you showed him the marks on your body, left by the nails when you were crucified, and he believed. You said then, 'Blessed are they that have not seen, and yet have believed'. Many people today say they don't believe in you because they can't see you. Please help them to realise that you are alive even if they can't see you, and help them to put their trust in you. Please help us too, when sometimes we doubt like Thomas did.

In your Name, Amen.

Lord Jesus, I think that the worst thing that can happen to anyone is for them to die. Sometimes when I think about dying it makes me feel afraid. When someone dies it's the end of their life and it means that we won't ever see them again. But you died, Lord Jesus, and then came back to life: a new life with a new body. When you were on earth you said, 'I am the Resurrection and the Life. Whoever believes in me shall never die. Because I live you shall live as well'.

Thank you that if we believe in you and trust you, we don't have to be afraid of dying because you will raise us from death to live with you in heaven. Thank you that instead of being the end of our lives, death will be the beginning of a wonderful new life in your presence.

Thank you for taking away my fear of death.

Amen.

I sometimes think about the cross,
And shut my eyes and try to see
The cruel nails and crown of thorns,
And Jesus crucified for me

Lord Jesus, However hard I try to imagine what it must have been like for you to die on the cross, I know I will never really understand all the pain and the loneliness you went through. Please help me to understand more, that I might be truly thankful to you for what you have done for me.

                              In your Name, Amen.

Lord Jesus, Sometimes when we read stories of what you did when you lived on earth it seems as though you were so perfect that you would never could have been sad or lonely or upset. But when we read about your death it helps us to see that you really do know all about suffering and because you have been through it, you understand our feelings when we are lonely or upset or suffering in any way. Thank you that it was because you loved us that you went through such awful suffering, and thank you for your help and love for us today when our lives are hard.

                              In your Name, Amen.

6   Ascension

At the name of Jesus 13

Philippians chapter 2 verses 5–11
John chapter 1 verses 1–14

Christ triumphant 25

Acts chapter 1 verses 1–11
Isaiah chapter 53 verses 1–12

Jesus Christ is alive today 129

1 Corinthians chapter 15 verses 12–26
Colossians chapter 1 verses 9–19
Ephesians chapter 3 verses 14–19

Our eyes have seen the glory 191

Acts chapter 1 verses 1–11
Ephesians chapter 1 verses 15–23

Prayers for Ascension

Dear Lord Jesus, If I had been one of your disciples when you were on earth, I think I would have loved you very much because you were such a good person, and I would have been very sad when you left to go back to heaven. The disciples must have been lonely without you there as their friend. But I suppose it was a good thing that you left them because now You are in heaven You can send the Holy Spirit to be with everyone who asks, and now everyone all over the world can be your friend; not just those who knew you when you were on earth. Please send your Holy Spirit to us to teach us more about you so that we might love you more and more.

In your Name, Amen.

Dear Lord Jesus, Sometimes I wonder where you live now: we can't see you and yet we can talk to you when we pray, and we know that you see us and look after us. This morning's Bible story tells how you went back to heaven after you had risen from the dead. Even though I can't see heaven and don't know where it is thank you that you have promised that if we put our trust in you now, we will come to live in heaven with you when we die. I'm looking forward to that. Please teach me to trust you more each day.

In your Name, Amen.

Dear Lord Jesus, It seems that when you lived on earth you did so much good, helping people, making sick people well, teaching about God, but now you have gone back to be with your Father in Heaven. Thank you that even though you don't live with us on earth any more, you still care for us: the Bible tells us that you pray for us and that you send the Holy Spirit to be our Comforter and Teacher. Now you live in heaven it is up to us to show people your love and to help them as you would. Please help us to be good witnesses of you to those around us.

In your Name, Amen.

7   Pentecost (Whitsun)

All over the world   5   Isaiah chapter 11 verses 1–9
                           Joel chapter 2 verses 23–32

For I'm building a   Ephesians chapter 2 verses 11–22
   people of power   47   Psalm 149
                           John chapter 17 verses 1, 13–23
                           Matthew chapter 16 verses 13–20

God whose son   62   Acts chapter 2
                           1 Corinthians chapter 12 verses
                              1–11

Spirit of the living   Acts chapter 2
   God   222   Acts chapter 19 verses 1–6
                           John chapter 14 verses 15–26

Prayers at Pentecost

Lord Jesus, When you left the disciples to go back to heaven, you promised that the Holy Spirit would be sent to be with all who believed in you, to teach them more about you and to help them become like you. Today we remember the day that your Holy Spirit came to the disciples and changed their lives. Thank you that you still send the Holy Spirit to all those who believe in you so that we can learn more about you and have our lives changed.

In your Name, Amen.

Lord Jesus, When you lived on earth you allowed the Holy Spirit to fill your life and work through you. Now that you are in heaven, the Church is your body on earth and just like you, all Christians need to let your Holy Spirit fill them and work through them so that the Church can do all the things that you did, and help many people. We pray that you will help us to give you our lives so that we will be channels for your Holy Spirit to work through.

We ask this for your sake, Amen.

Dear God, When we think of you we often think about churches as well. But before the day of Pentecost there wasn't a church; just a group of disciples who believed in the Lord Jesus. At Pentecost you sent the Holy Spirit to live within each of the disciples so that they would be joined together as one: the first church. It's so sad that today many Christians argue and are separated from each other: we pray that your Spirit will unite us and make us one as the first Christians were. Please help us to be part of that, living at peace with each other, and learning how to love one another.

In Jesus' Name, Amen.

Heavenly Father, We praise you for all that happened on the day of Pentecost when your Holy Spirit came upon Jesus' disciples and formed them into your Church. Thank you for the power He gave them to speak in many languages so that people from different countries understand all they said about the Lord Jesus and believed in Him. Thank you that your Holy Spirit is able to work today just as He did then, giving to Christians different gifts and abilities to help them tell others about Jesus.

We pray that you will use each one of our lives to let others know about Jesus, so that more people might come to believe in Him.

In Jesus' Name, Amen.

Lord Jesus, Pentecost was a very special day because before that day the Jews and Gentiles were always separate in every way, but at Pentecost you sent your Spirit to bring Jews and Gentiles together into the Church. Thank you that you can take two groups of people who are so different and make them one in the Lord Jesus.

Please help us to learn how we can be at peace and in unity with all people when we are one in you.

In your Name, Amen.

Heavenly Father, We praise you that when you had sent Jesus to die on the cross so we could be forgiven and made clean, you then sent the Holy Spirit to live in those people who accept your forgiveness. We pray that today you would forgive us for those things in our lives that are wrong, make us clean from those wrong things and fill us with your Holy

Spirit so that we might have your power to live differently from now on, and that we might be your witnesses to those around us.

For your Sake, Amen.

Dear God, Thank you for the story of how the church began by the Holy Spirit coming to live in those who believed in Jesus. We know that now Jesus is in heaven the church is meant to be like your body here on earth, helping others and telling them about Him. Thank you for the churches today that are like that, and we pray for them and their leaders that they will help many people come to know Jesus.

Thank you for those in our churches who teach us about the Lord Jesus; we pray that you will help them in their work.

In Jesus' Name, Amen.

8   Harvest

Come you thankful people, come   32
Exodus chapter 23 verses 14–19
John chapter 4 verses 31–38

For the beauty of the earth   48
Genesis chapter 1 verses 1–31
2 Peter chapter 1 verses 3–9
Psalm 8

God whose farm is all creation   61
Psalm 24
Matthew chapter 13 verses 1–23
Haggai chapter 1 verses 5–7

God who made the earth   63
Genesis chapter 1 verses 1–31
2 Peter chapter 1 verses 3–9

Great is your faithfulness   64
Psalm 65
Lamentations chapter 3 verses 22–26
Genesis chapter 8 verse 20, chapter 9 verse 17
Exodus chapter 16 verses 1–36, chapter 17 verses 1–7

I have seen the golden sunshine   99
Matthew chapter 13 verses 24–30
Matthew chapter 13 verses 36–43

Jesus is Lord!   137
Genesis chapter 1 verses 1–31
Psalm 111 verses 2–10

Now the green blade rises   174
Matthew chapter 13 verses 1–23

Now thank we all our God   175
Ruth chapter 2 verses 17–23
Matthew chapter 13 verses 1–23
Psalm 111 verses 2–10

Our harvest day is over   193
1 Timothy chapter 6 verses 17–19
Psalm 111 verses 2–10
Psalm 65

Someone's brought a loaf of bread   220
John chapter 6 verses 1–14
Mark chapter 6 verses 30–44

Think of a world
  without any
  flowers   254

Yes, God is good   293

Genesis chapter 1 verses 1–31
Psalm 104

Genesis chapter 1 verses 1–31
Psalm 145 verses 3–9

Prayers for Harvest

Dear Lord God, At this time of harvest when we remember all that you have provided for us we also want to pray for those people in countries where there is so little to eat. We don't understand why we have so much when they have so little, but we ask that you will teach us to share what we have and show us ways to help others wherever we can. Please help us not to become greedy and selfish, Keeping everything for ourselves but always to be ready to share generously with those in need because we know that is what you would do.

We ask it for Jesus' sake, Amen.

Dear Heavenly Father, At this special time of year we want to think about the way you provide food for us, and to say 'thank you' for all that you give to us. You are the one who makes the sun shine, and the rain fall; you are the one who makes the plants grow and who gives animals life. Everything that we eat has come from you and is a gift to us, and we thank you. Thank you for giving us more than enough, and thank you for giving us such variety so that food is never boring. Please help us to appreciate all that we have and be grateful for it.

In Jesus' Name, Amen.

Dear Heavenly Father, Sometimes we think that miracles only happened to people in the Bible, but every year the harvest is one of your greatest miracles – please forgive us that when we get used to something happening every year we forget to see it as being special each time. We praise you for the miracle of grass growing from seed, of wheat and barley coming from grain, of apple trees coming from tiny pips and then producing their own fruit. We praise you for the miracle of the way a tree draws in water through its roots and then turns it into fruitjuice that we can enjoy; for the cows who chew grass all day and then produce milk which we use in so many ways; and for the bees drawing up nectar from flowers and turning it into honey.

Dear Lord, this world is full of miracles and we praise you for each one.

In Jesus' Name, Amen.

Dear God, When I try to decide what my most favourite food is, it's usually impossible: there's so much to choose from and it depends on what mood I'm in, whether it's a hot or cold day, and who's cooking. But thank you that there are so many different things to choose from and that we don't have to eat the same food every-day like they do in some countries. Thank you that there is always plenty to eat in this country and that there are not thousands of people without food as there are in some parts of the world. Please forgive us for the times when we complain about our food: help us to see how wrong that is and please teach us to be thankful to you.

In Jesus' Name, Amen.

Dear Lord, One thing always amazes me about your creation, that however many colours there are around in flowers, trees, or fruit, they always go together. Thank you for colours and for putting them together so well.

Amen

Lord, When we go to a supermarket and see all the food packaged up in tins and boxes, it's hard to remember that it all came from things that you created. Thank you for the people who work in factories and shops to provide us with things to eat. We pray that as they work they might remember that you made the food they work with, and be grateful to you for giving them a job.

Amen.

Heavenly Father, At this time of harvest we especially want to remember the farmers in our prayers. We thank you for them and the work they do. Often they have to work very hard and very long hours looking after their animals and growing the crops. We pray for the farmers in our area and ask you to look after them.

In Jesus' Name, Amen.

Lord, Thank you for the seasons of the year. They make the year so much more interesting. There are nice things about all the seasons and each one of them is necessary for the harvest. Just to see the way the seasons come and go in the same order each year reminds us of your faithfulness to us and the way you constantly provide for all that we need.

Thank you Lord, Amen.

9 God the Father

Abba Father   2

Romans chapter 8 verses 14–17
Mark chapter 14 verses 32–42
Matthew chapter 6 verses 5–15
Genesis chapter 11 verse 28, chapter 12 verse 9
Genesis chapter 22 verses 1–17

Be still and know that I am God   22

Psalm 46
John chapter 14 verses 23–27
Luke chapter 8 verses 22–25
Luke chapter 10 verses 38–42

Dear Lord and Father of mankind   37

Romans chapter 12 verses 1–8
Matthew chapter 4 verses 18–22
Genesis chapter 27 verses 1–46

Father, hear the prayer we offer   41

Luke chapter 22 verses 39–46
Mark chapter 1 verses 35–39
Genesis chapter 39 verses 1–23
Daniel chapter 6 verses 1–24

Father I place into your hands   42

Psalm 25
Psalm 139
Deuteronomy chapter 33 verses 26–29
Matthew chapter 6 verses 25–34

Father, lead me day by day   43

Luke chapter 4 verses 1–14
Mark chapter 1 verses 9–13
Exodus chapter 14 verses 1–31

Father, we adore you   44

Psalm 95
John chapter 14 verses 21–26
John 12 verses 1–8
Daniel chapter 3 verses 1–28
Acts chapter 6 verses 9–15, chapter 7 verses 1–54

Father, we love you   45

John chapter 12 verses 23–32
Psalm chapter 86 verses 1–12
John chapter 16 verses 7–16

God is so good   53
Psalm 116
John chapter 8 verses 31–36
Luke chapter 8 verses 26–39

God is good   55
Psalm 100 verses 1–5
Hebrews chapter 4 verses 14–16
Psalm chapter 34 verses 1–10

God is our guide   56
Psalm 25 verses 4–15
Jude chapters 20–25
Proverbs chapter 3 verses 1–13
Psalm 27
Exodus chapter 13 verses 17–22

God is working His purpose out   57
Isaiah chapter 11 verses 1–10
Isaiah chapter 55 verses 6–11
1 Thessalonians chapter 4 verse 13, chapter 5 verse 11
Jonah (extracts)

God's not dead   60
Ephesians chapter 3 verses 14–19
Luke chapter 24 verses 1–12

Great is your faithfulness   64
Psalm 45
Lamentations chapter 3 verses 22–26
Genesis chapter 8 verse 20, chapter 9 verse 17
Psalm 19
Exodus chapter 16 verses 1–36, chapter 17 verses 1–7

Hallelujah for the Lord our God   66
Revelation chapter 19 verses 4–7
Psalm 9 verses 7–11
Daniel chapter 3 verses 1–28
1 Kings chapter 18 verses 17–40

He brought me to his banqueting house   73
Song of songs chapter 2 verses 1–4
Matthew chapter 22 verses 1–14
John chapter 6 verses 1–14
John chapter 6 verses 43–58

He's got the whole wide world in His hands 78

Psalm 24
Genesis chapter 8 verse 21, chapter 9 verse 17
Deuteronomy chapter 33 verses 26–29

He's great, He's God 79

Colossians chapter 1 verses 9–19
Luke chapter 1 verses 30–33, 46–55
John chapter 14 verses 1–6

How great is our God 82

Exodus chapter 15 verses 1–8
Psalm 139 verses 7–10
Isaiah chapter 13 verses 15–19

How lovely on the mountains 84

Isaiah chapter 52 verses 7–10
Revelation chapter 19 verses 4–7
Isaiah chapter 54 verses 1–14
Matthew chapter 28 verses 16–20

I am so glad that my Father in Heaven 88

John chapter 15 verses 9–17
Luke chapter 15 verses 1–7
John chapter 14 verses 16–26

I'm very glad of God 107

Colossians chapter 1 verses 15–20
Psalm 95 verses 1–8

Let us praise God together 152

John chapter 17 verses 1–5
2 Timothy verses 1–10

Let us with a gladsome mind 154

Psalm 104
Psalm 118
Genesis chapter 1 verses 1–27

My God is so big 169

Luke chapter 1 verse 37
Romans chapter 8 verses 28–39
Exodus chapter 14 verses 13–31
Luke chapter 8 verses 22–25

Now thank we all our God 175

Psalm 95 verses 1–7
Colossians chapter 1 verses 15–20
Luke chapter 17 verses 11–19

O Lord my God 179	Psalm 8 Romans chapter 5 verses 9–11 1 Thessalonians chapter 4 verses 16–17 John chapter 3 verses 16–18
Our Father who is in Heaven 192	Matthew chapter 6 verses 9–15 Luke chapter 11 verses 1–13
Praise God from whom all blessings flow 199	Psalm 67 verses 3–7 Psalm 145 verses 1–7 Psalm 100
Praise to the Lord our God 205	Psalm 47 Psalm 34 verses 1–10 Ephesians chapter 5 verses 1, 15–21
Stand up and bless the Lord 224	Nehemiah chapter 9 verses 5b, 17, 31 Psalm 111 verses 1–10 Luke chapter 15 verses 11–32
The joy of the Lord is my strength 240	Acts chapter 3 verses 1–8 Philippians chapter 4 verses 4–9 Nehemiah chapter 8 verses 1–12
The King of love my shepherd is 241	Psalm 23 John chapter 10 verses 1–21
The Lord's my shepherd 243	Luke chapter 15 verses 1–7
The Lord is my shepherd 244	As for No's 241 and 243
The steadfast love of the Lord 250	Lamentations chapter 3 verses 22–24 Romans chapter 8 verses 35–39 Genesis chapter 18 verses 17–22

To God be the   John chapter 3 verses 1–17
  glory   259   John chapter 14 verses 1–14
                         Romans chapter 8 verses 1–11
                         Luke chapter 5 verses 16–26

Yes, God is good   293   Psalm 65
                         Psalm 19
                         Ephesians chapter 1 verses 3–14

Prayers to God the Father

Dear God, It's wonderful to know that you are such a loving
heavenly Father to us. Thank you that all you want to do in
our lives is to show us your love and your goodness. There
are lots of people who don't know that though. Often they
blame you for the bad things in the world without thanking
you for the good things you give us. Please help us all to
understand that we will only really enjoy this earth and our
lives if we live the way you want us to.

In Jesus' Name, Amen.

Dear Lord God, Sometimes I wonder however you can know
everything about all the people in this world. There are so
many people and many of them live so far apart. How do
you manage to see us all at the same time and listen to all
our prayers? Thank you that you do even if I don't understand how, and thank you that it is possible for every person
in the world to know you because you speak to them all
through your creation, through their conscience, and
through your Word, the Bible. It's sad that when you speak
to people so many don't bother to listen. Please help us to
take time to listen to you and to get to know you better.

In Jesus' Name, Amen.

Dear Heavenly Father, Thank you that I can trust you. It's
not always easy to trust people: sometimes I've told my
friends a secret and they have told other people, or someone
has promised to help me and then forgotten their promise.
But I know that *you* will never let me down: wherever I am
and whatever I am doing, you are there with me. Please help

me to trust you more, and to learn to do the things that please you in my life.

                    In Jesus' Name, Amen.

Dear God, I don't know anyone else who cares for me the way you do. Thank you that your Love for me never stops: you don't ever sleep, so even at night when I feel afraid you are still looking after me, and whenever I feel lonely, you are with me and caring for me.

                    Thank you for being my friend, Amen.

Dear God, There's a question my friends say they keep asking: 'Do you exist, and how can I prove it if you do?' I don't know what to tell them. Of course I know you exist; I know how you live in my heart, and how sometimes, when I'm alone I'm aware of you being with me; but how can I make *them* understand? Will you do it Lord; help them to believe, help them to know for themselves how good it is to be loved by you and to belong to you.

                    Thank you Lord, Amen.

Dear God, Sometimes we think that it is the leaders of different countries who control what is happening in the world, and then we can get scared because it seems as though things could so easily go wrong. But thank you that your Word tells us that the Lord Jesus is actually reigning as king over all the earth; that He is bringing people to Himself so that they will know His justice and peace; and one day all the nations on earth will recognise Jesus as their king. Thank you that because we know this we don't have to be afraid of the future, but can be glad at what God is doing in the world today. Thank you for being in control of the world.

                    Amen.

Dear God, Can anyone really know everything that there is to know? I suppose if that person had made everything that exists they would know all about it. And that's you Lord. You could answer every question I have about this world, and people, and things that happen. But you don't. You leave some of my questions unanswered. Perhaps my mind is too small for some of the answers, and I need to leave those questions with you. Please help me to do so.

                    Amen.

Heavenly Father, It's a wonderful thing to know that we belong to you and have your promise that you will always be with us and always care for us. It's even more special when we remember that we belong to you twice over: once because you created us, and twice because Jesus died to buy us back for you after we had gone off on our own way instead of living as you wanted us to. Thank you for being our creator and our Father.

Amen.

Dear God, We thank you that because Jesus died for us you want to adopt us into your family and make us your children. Thank you that when we become your children, Jesus becomes our brother, and we can share with Him everything that you have given to Him. Thank you that as your children we inherit eternal life and all the riches of your kingdom! Please help us to appreciate all that you have given to us now: thank you that we don't have to wait until we go to heaven to enjoy what you have given to us, but that even here on earth we can know that we are your children and enjoy all the goodness that you give to us.

In Jesus' Name, Amen.

Dear God, You wrote one of the ten commandments especially for children: 'Honour your father and mother'. We know that we don't always keep that commandment and we're sorry. You gave us our parents and they have given us so much: thank you for them. We pray for them today that you will help them as they look after us, and ask that you will teach us to obey them and be helpful to them.

For your Sake, Amen.

Dear Heavenly Father, Thank you that you are not a God that we have to be afraid of, but a God who wants us to know how much you love us and who wants us to enjoy singing your praises. We have so much to say thank you for: please help us to do so with our songs and also by the way we live; serving you with our lives.

In Jesus' Name, Amen.

You make me feel important, God,
you have shown me that,
so far as you are concerned,
I matter.

I matter so much to you
that you allowed Jesus to be put to death
for my sake.

That just amazes me
and I don't really understand love like that,
it's beyond me.

Feeling *that* important is good.
Thank you for the value you place upon me.

Would it be possible for me to see things
through your eyes?
If I could I'd most likely value my family
and my friends more highly.
Help me to love people like you do, or,
if that isn't possible,
help me to love them
more than I do now.
Please.

Loving Father, We thank you for all the goodness you have
shown to us in our lives by providing all the things we need
to live. We thank you most of all that you have made it
possible for us to know you as our heavenly Father and as
our friend, and that you will look after us all the days of our
life. Please help us to get to know you better so that we will
grow to love you more and more.

We ask this in Jesus' Name, Amen.

Dear Heavenly Father, You are the only one who really
understands how I feel; the things that make me happy and
the things that make me sad. Thank you that you care about
the way I feel and even when I feel that no one else cares or
understands, I know that you are with me and you will help
me. It seems so strange that you can care for everyone on

earth at the same time. I find it difficult to care about the people I know and who love me, but please teach me how to love them more.

In Jesus' Name, Amen.

Dear God, All the people that I know can change so easily: one day they are happy, the next they may be sad or unhappy, one day they are kind to me and the next day it seems as though they don't really care. It's because they all have so much else to think about apart from me. Thank you God, that you never change – you'll always be the same from one day to the next; always loving me, and always wanting the best for me. It makes me feel so safe to know that.

Thank you, Amen.

Dear God, Thank you that you love children. Thank you that yours is a very special love; you love us even more than a father loves his own children, because you made us and we belong to you. Thank you for showing us how much you love us by letting Jesus die on the cross for us so that we can now get to know you as our Heavenly Father.

Thank you God, Amen.

We praise you Lord because you are the creator of the world. We praise you because you are such a great God, and you are able to do so many wonderful things that no man could ever do however clever he was. Thank you that you give to us all that we need to live, and thank you that although you are such a great God, you care about each one of us because we are your children.

In Jesus' Name, Amen.

Dear Father, Thank you that you are a kind and a loving God. Thank you that you always look after us and care about us. Sometimes we have to move away from people whom we love and then we miss them and are sad. Sometimes the people that we love make us sad because they say or do something that hurts us. Thank you that you are not like that; you will never leave us and you will never hurt us because you will love us in a way that people can't. Help us to learn to love others in the way you do and to be a good friend to them.

In Jesus' Name, Amen.

Dear Heavenly Father, I thank you that you never give up knocking at the door of our lives. We get so wrapped up in all the things that we do each day that we never hear you knocking. Help us to be still and listen, and to open the door to you. You have promised, Lord, that if we invite you into our lives then you make us into the people that you intend us to be.

Thank you Lord, Amen.

10   Jesus

A boy gave to Jesus five loaves and two fish   1

Luke chapter 9 verses 10–17
Mark chapter 6 verses 3–44

Alleluia, Alleluia, give thanks to the risen Lord   3

Romans chapter 6 verses 3–10
Matthew chapter 28 verses 1–10

At the name of Jesus   13

Philippians chapter 2 verses 5–11
Colossians chapter 1 verses 9–22
Acts chapter 1 verses 1–11
Ephesians chapter 1 verse 15, chapter 2 verse 10

Bless the Lord, O my soul   19

Psalm 103
Revelation chapter 19 verses 1–9
Mark chapter 11 verses 1–11

Blessed assurance   20

1 John chapter 1 verse 5, chapter 2 verse 2
Colossians chapter 3 verses 1–17
John chapter 3 verses 1–17

By blue Galilee   23

John chapter 4 verses 43–54
Mark chapter 4 verses 1–9
Luke chapter 4 verses 14 & 15

Christ triumphant   25

John chapter 1 verses 1–14
Isaiah chapter 52 verses 1–12
Hebrews chapter 10 verses 1–23
Revelation chapter 4 verses 1–11

Come to Jesus, He's amazing   33

Mark chapter 10 verses 13–16
Luke chapter 18 verses 15–18

Come and praise the Lord our king   34

Luke chapter 2 verses 8–14
Ephesians chapter 1 verse 15, chapter 2 verse 10
John chapter 14 verses 1–19

Do you want a Pilot? 40	Luke chapter 8 verses 22–25 Ecclesiastes chapter 11 verse 9, chapter 12 verse 7 John chapter 10 verses 1–14, 27–30
Father, we adore you 44	Psalm 95 John chapter 14 verses 21–26 John chapter 12 verses 1–8
Father, we love you 45	John chapter 12 verses 23–32 Psalm 86 verses 1–2 John chapter 16 verses 7–16
Follow me says Jesus 46	John chapter 10 verses 1–18, 25–29 Psalm 23
God sent His Son 58	Luke chapter 24 verses 1–49 Luke chapter 19 verses 1–10 John chapter 14 verses 15–26
Happiness is to know the Saviour 70	2 Corinthians chapter 5 verses 11–21 Luke chapter 5 verses 16–26 Psalm 16
He is Lord 75	Acts chapter 2 verses 34–36 Philippians chapter 2 verses 5–11 1 Corinthians chapter 15 verses 25–27 Revelation chapter 19 verses 1–9
I am trusting you Lord Jesus 86	John chapter 14 verses 1–6, 15–21 Psalm 25 Proverbs chapter 3 verses 1–7 Luke chapter 8 verses 41–56
I am the way, the truth and the life 89	John chapter 14 verses 1–10 John chapter 11 verses 1–15, 21–27 1 John chapter 1 verse 1, chapter 2 verse 2 Luke chapter 12 verses 16–21

In the name of
  Jesus   111

Luke chapter 4 verses 1–13
1 John chapter 5 verses 1–5
Matthew chapter 8 verses 28–34

I serve a risen
  Saviour   113

Matthew chapter 28 verses 1–9
John chapter 11 verses 1–27
Romans chapter 5 verses 1–10
Hebrews chapter 5 verses 5a–8

I was lost but Jesus
  found me   125

Luke chapter 15 verses 3–7
Luke chapter 15 verses 8–10
Luke chapter 15 verses 11–32

I will sing the
  wondrous
  story   127

Luke chapter 15 verses 1–7
John chapter 5 verses 19–30
John chapter 20 verses 24–31

Jesus bids us
  shine   128

Luke chapter 11 verses 33–36
John chapter 1 verses 1–12
John chapter 8 verse 12
Isaiah chapter 59 verses 1–2, 8–10,
  chapter 60 verses 1–3

Jesus Christ is alive
  today   129

1 Corinthians chapter 15 verses
  12–26
Colossians chapter 1 verses 9–19
Ephesians chapter 3 verses 14–19

Jesus Christ is risen
  today   130

Luke chapter 24 verses 1–12
Hebrews chapter 11 verses 1–6
Romans chapter 5 verses 1–11

Jesus died for all the
  children   132

John chapter 3 verses 14–17
Mark chapter 10 verses 13–16

Jesus, how lovely you
  are   133

Revelation chapter 22 verses 1–17
Luke chapter 24 verses 1–12
Revelation chapter 19 verses 1–9

Jesus' hands were kind
  hands   134

John chapter 9 verses 1–34
Mark chapter 1 verses 40–45
Mark chapter 10 verses 13–16

Jesus is a friend of   John chapter 15 verses 12–17
   mine   136   John chapter 11 verses 1–44
                              Romans chapter 5 verses 1–11

Jesus is Lord!   137   Colossians chapter 1 verses 9–20
                              Romans chapter 1 verses 18–20
                              Psalm 19

Jesus' love is very   John chapter 15 verses 9–17
   wonderful   139   1 John chapter 4 verses 7–10
                              Ephesians chapter 3 verses 14–21
                              Luke chapter 15 verses 11–32

Jesus loves me!   140   John chapter 3 verses 1–17
                              Mark chapter 10 verses 13–16
                              John chapter 14 verses 1–6
                              Luke chapter 8 verses 41–56

Jesus, Name above all   Philippians chapter 2 verses 5–11
   names   141   Isaiah chapter 9 verses 2, 6–7
                              Acts chapter 3 verses 1–16
                              Ephesians chapter 1 verses 15–23

King of kings and Lord   Revelation chapter 4 verses 1–11
   of lords   148   Mark chapter 1 verses 1–11
                              Luke chapter 1 verses 26–33

Let's talk about   John chapter 14 verses 1–6
   Jesus   150   John chapter 10 verses 1–9
                              Ephesians chapter 1 verses 15–23

Led like a lamb   151   Luke chapter 22 verses 22–65
                              Luke chapter 22 verse 66, chapter
                                 23 verse 25
                              Matthew chapter 28 verses 1–10
                              Luke chapter 24 verses 13–32

Lord Jesus Christ   156   1 John chapter 1 verse 5, chapter
                                 2 verse 5
                              Matthew chapter 6 verses 1–18
                              1 Corinthians chapter 11 verses
                                 23–32
                              Romans chapter 12 verses 1–21

Lord of all   Mark chapter 10 verses 13–16
  hopefulness   157   Psalm 121
                            Romans chapter 8 verses 28–39
                            Luke chapter 8 verses 22–25

Majesty   160   Philippians chapter 2 verses 5–11
                            Acts chapter 2 verses 14, 22–36
                            Revelation chapter 1 verses 9–18
                            Revelation chapter 4 verses 1–11

May the mind of Christ   Philippians chapter 2 verses 1–11
  my Saviour   165   Psalm 1
                            Psalm 119 verses 1–16
                            John chapter 14 verses 23–28

My Lord is higher   170   Psalm 18 verses 1–6, 16–36
                            Mark chapter 6 verses 45–52
                            Job chapter 38 verses 1–41

Oh, oh, oh how good   Acts chapter 3 verses 1–16
  is the Lord   180   Ephesians chapter 1 verses 3–14
                            Psalm 103

On Calvary's tree he   Luke chapter 23 verses 26–46
  died for me   183   John chapter 8 verses 31–36

Our eyes have seen the   Acts chapter 1 verses 1–11
  glory   191   Ephesians chapter 1 verses 15–23

Praise Him, praise   Luke chapter 24 verses 1–49
  Him, Jesus our   Psalm 61
  blessed   Mark chapter 10 verses 13–16
  redeemer   203

Praise my soul   204   Revelation chapter 4 verses 1–11
                            Hebrews chapter 2 verses 9–18
                            Luke chapter 5 verses 16–26

Saviour of the   Luke chapter 22 verses 39–53
  world   216   Luke chapter 23 verses 33–49

Sing we the King   218

John chapter 1 verses 14–34
Psalm 24
Isaiah chapter 11 verses 1–10

Soon and very
   soon   221

Matthew chapter 24 verses 36–50
John chapter 14 verses 1–4
Mark chapter 13 verses 32–37

Tell me the old, old
   story   227

John chapter 3 verses 16–21
Colossians chapter 1 verses 9–23
Ephesians chapter 1 verses 3–14

Tell me the stories of
   Jesus   228

Luke chapter 10 verses 25–37
Luke chapter 15 verses 11–32
Matthew chapter 26 verses 36–46
Mark chapter 10 verses 13–16
Matthew chapter 28 verses 1–10

Thank you, thank you,
   Jesus   231

John chapter 20 verses 19–29
Romans chapter 8 verses 28–39
Ephesians chapter 5 verses 18–21

Turn your eyes upon
   Jesus   260

Colossians chapter 3 verses 1–17
Luke chapter 9 verses 27–36
Revelation chapter 1 verses 9–18

We have a king who
   rides on a
   donkey   264

Matthew chapter 21 verses 1–11
Luke chapter 19 verses 28–44

We love to praise you,
   Jesus   265

John chapter 15 verses 1–17
John chapter 10 verses 1–18
Luke chapter 13 verses 22–30

What a friend we have
   in Jesus   273

Matthew chapter 6 verses 25–34
John chapter 15 verses 1–17
Luke chapter 11 verses 1–13
Psalm 62

What a wonderful
   Saviour is
   Jesus   274

Philippians chapter 2 verses 1–11
1 Thessalonians chapter 4 verses
   13–18

When the Lord in glory   1 Thessalonians chapter 4 verses
   comes   280   13–18
                                 Revelation chapter 1 verses 9–18
                                 1 John chapter 2 verse 28, chapter
                                    3 verse 3

Who took fish and   Matthew chapter 14 verses 15–21
   bread?   286   John chapter 9 verses 1–34
                                 Mark chapter 10 verses 13–16

Yesterday, today,   Hebrews chapter 13 verses 1–9
   forever   294   Hebrews chapter 1 verses 1–12
                                 2 Peter chapter 3 verses 1–12
                                 Colossians chapter 2 verses 4–10

You are the king of   Isaiah chapter 9 verses 1, 6–7
   glory   296   Revelation chapter 4 verses 1–11
                                 Hebrews chapter 1 verses 1–12
                                 John chapter 6 verses 61–69

Jesus Prayers

Dear Lord God, Sometimes I wonder why Jesus had to die.
It seems so sad that a man who never did any wrong was
put to death like a criminal. And you could have saved Him,
God. The night before He died, Jesus prayed that if it was
possible He wanted to avoid death, but you let Him go on.
Do you really love me enough to let Jesus die for me? That
makes me want to love you; please teach me to.

                                                 Amen.

Dear God, Sometimes I wonder why it's so important to
know about you: to learn about the Bible, and come to church
or school assemblies; but thank you that the hymns we sing,
and the stories we read remind us of why we need to know
you: because of your love for us. Thank you that Jesus died
for each one of us so that we could be forgiven for all the
wrong things we have done.

Thank you that you were willing to give up your life for me: please help me to love you because of what you have done for me.

> In Jesus' Name, Amen.

Dear Lord Jesus, Sometimes we give people nicknames, names that tell us something about that person: sometimes the names aren't very nice and can make that person unhappy. Please help us to remember not to hurt others by giving them unkind names.

In the Bible, you are given many names that tell us different things about you. You are called the 'Shepherd', 'Light of the World', 'Saviour', 'Friend' and many others. All your names make you sound the kind of person I would like to know. Please help me to know you better in my life.

> In your Name, Amen.

Dear Lord Jesus, Although we hear of many special people you are the most important because it is by knowing you that we can have our sins forgiven and come to live in heaven when we die. Thank you that you are not just a name, or someone very far away, but you are 'Emmanuel', God with us: our friend wherever we are and whatever we are doing. It's strange to think that you can be with each one of us at the same time, but thank you that that is possible because you are God.

> Amen.

Dear Lord Jesus, Thank you that when you were on earth you loved children and spent time with them. It's good to know that each one of us is important to you even though we sometimes don't feel very special. Please teach us to love you while we are still children so that as we grow up we will know you as our friend and you will be able to use our lives to tell others about your love.

> In your Name, Amen.

Lord Jesus, In some ways our lives are a bit like houses, with windows that we can see out of and a door through which we let people come into our lives to be our friends. Help us to realise that you stand at the door of our lives, knocking, and wanting to be let in. Sometimes we are so busy we don't

even hear you, and other times we hear but don't want to
let you in because we want to keep our lives to ourselves.
When we don't hear you, please make us stop and take time
to listen, and when we choose to ignore you, please remind
us that you have a right to be involved in our lives because
you made us, and gave us our life.

Come into our lives today, Lord Jesus, and make us your
home.

In your Name, Amen.

Why do you care about me?
I'm not worth it.
I'm rotten.
I can't seem to do the right thing, ever.
Why should anyone love me,
especially you, Lord?
I feel worthless.

Yet –
my mind keeps coming back to you.
(That's probably why I'm praying.)

If human beings were perfect
we wouldn't need you.
You said you came to earth to live and die
for sinners.
Well, I'm definitely a sinner.
If that gives me some value in your eyes, Lord,
thank you.
I can't understand that,
but I really want to believe it.

You're incredible, Lord,
fantastic!
So great, so mind-boggling,
so far beyond understanding, and yet
you came to earth as a baby,
grew to be a man,
but more than just a man,
no mere man could be as great as you are.
And then,
you who can never die chose to submit to death

for the best and the worst in me:
to encourage the best
and transform the worst.
You amaze me, you make me wonder;
and you have given me the gift of faith
which makes the unbelievable believable,
Thank you.

Lord Jesus, Thank you that you are totally trustworthy. Often in this world we get hurt by people or let down by them and we begin to think we can't put our trust in anyone. Thank you that you never let us down. Thank you that you never change. Help each of us to learn to trust you for every bit of our lives – even the thing which may seem impossible, or we may think you're not interested in.

Forgive us when we spend time worrying about things, simply because we have refused to hand them over to you.

In your Name, Amen.

Dear Lord Jesus, There are so many religions in the world; I find it hard sometimes to explain to my friends why they need to know You to know God. Thank you that we can be really sure that you are God's son because you rose from the dead and no one else has the power to do that. You are in heaven reigning as the king of kings and Lord of lords; please help my friends to accept you as *their* Lord and *their* Saviour.

In your Name, Amen.

Lord Jesus, We thank you that you are the light of the world, and that you want your light to shine all through the world so that people might come to know you and be part of your Kingdom of Light instead of living in darkness. Thank you that when we come to know you, you come to live in our lives and so we have your light within us. Please help us to let that light shine brightly for you so people know that we belong to you. Please forgive us for the things that we have done that were wrong that have stopped our lives being lights for you. Thank you that you can make our lives clean again so that your light can shine out from us.

In Jesus' Name, Amen.

Lord Jesus, Just as the sun provides light for us to see by and to enjoy creation, so you want to be the light of our lives, helping us to see all that God has done for us, and helping us to find the right path for our lives. We ask that you will teach us to follow you: the light of the world, and let you open our eyes to see all that you want to give us and do for us.

In your Name, Amen.

Lord Jesus, The Bible says that you are going to come back to this world one day and we know we can believe it, beause the Old Testament was right in so many ways about your coming for the first time.

It is exciting to know that no-one knows just when you will come back, but we are so glad that we can look forward to a time when you will bring this world to a close and there will be a new heaven and a new earth.

Thank you that when we know you, we have so much to look forward to.

Amen.

Dear Lord, When we look around at the world you made it seem sad that it has gone wrong in so many ways. People fighting each other and making each other unhappy; your creation spoilt as we destroy it in different ways. It's not like the world you planned at all, and it's all happened because men wouldn't listen to you and obey you even though this is your world.

Thank you that you aren't going to let it go on getting worse and worse until it falls apart, but you are going to come back to earth and restore it to what you intended it to be.Thank you that you want to restore us too, until we are the people you want us to be; reflections of yourself. We pray that we might put our lives right with you now so that when you do come again we will be part of your Kingdom.

In your Name, Amen.

Dear Father, Sometimes we forget who Jesus really is. To many people in the world He is just a name, but the Bible says that He is the Sovereign of the Universe and King over all this world. Please help us to respect and obey the Lord

Jesus as we would respect any earthly king, and also to worship him because He is God.

Please forgive us for the times we have used His name wrongly, and help us to make our lives an example for others to see how everyone should obey and honour the Lord Jesus.

In His Name, Amen.

Lord Jesus, It's hard to understand how when you came to earth you were God and yet were born and lived as a man. Although you were God, you put aside your glory and power and came only to do what your Father told you to, using the power that He gave to you by His Spirit. As you lived on earth, you showed by your character what God is like, and when you died, you made it possible for men to know God for themselves.

Thank you that you were willing to let go of your glory and power for our sakes, so that we might have an example of how to live our lives obediently and by the power of the Holy Spirit. When we find that hard to do, please help us to follow your example.

For your Sake, Amen.

Lord Jesus, The Bible says that it is by your power that this whole universe is held together and kept in order. Without you it would fall apart and there would be chaos. Our minds can't imagine what it would be like to be so powerful: you are so much greater than we can ever understand, and today we worship and praise you because you are Lord of this universe and everything belongs to you. You made us as part of your creation, help us to acknowledge you today as Lord of our lives and recognise that you are our God.

Amen.

Thank you, Jesus,
thanks ever so much
I asked you to help me and you have done.

It was confusing for a while,
I was all mixed up,
but you have opened my eyes;
I see!

I didn't know how to see good with so much evil about;
I didn't know how to see your way,
so obsessed was I with mine.
You have expanded my horizon,
you have extended my vision,
you have added colour and shape and beauty and light.
For the ability to see
thank you, Lord.

Lord Jesus, Thank you that if we belong to you we have nothing to be afraid of because you look after us as a shepherd looks after his sheep. Thank you that you will always provide what we need, you will always guide us and show us the right way to go, and then when we die you will take us to be with you in heaven. Please help us to trust you more and to follow you more closely as a sheep follows its shepherd.

We ask this in your Name, Amen.

11 The Holy Spirit

All over the world 5

Isaiah chapter 11 verses 1–9
Joel chapter 2 verses 23–32

For I'm building a
  people of power 47

Ephesians chapter 2 verses 11–22
Psalm 149
John chapter 17 verses 1, 13–23
Matthew chapter 16 verses 13–20

Give me oil in my
  lamp 50

Matthew chapter 25 verses 1–13
Zachariah chapter 1 verses 1–14
John chapter 14 verses 15–26

God whose Son 62

Acts chapter 2
1 Corinthians chapter 12 verses
  1–11

I am a lighthouse 87

Matthew chapter 5 verses 13–16
Luke chapter 8 verses 22–25
Zachariah chapter 1 verses 1–14

I want to walk with
  Jesus Christ 124

Luke chapter 14 verses 25–33
1 John chapter 1 verses 5–10
Philippians chapter 2 verses 5–16

Love, joy, peace and
  patience 158

Galatians chapter 5 verses 16–26
Romans chapter 5 verses 1–5
Romans chapter 8 verses 1–14
John chapter 15 verses 1–8

Spirit of the living
  God 222

Acts chapter 2
Acts chapter 19 verses 1–6
John chapter 14 verses 15–26
Psalm 51

Thank you God for
  sending Jesus 233

John chapter 14 verses 23–27
1 Peter chapter 1 verses 13–21
John chapter 16 verses 5–15

This is the day   255   Psalm 118
                             Genesis chapter 1 verses 1–8
                             Acts chapter 2
                             Matthew chapter 28 verses 1–9

Though the world has   Matthew chapter 7 verses 13–20
  forsaken God   257   John chapter 13 verses 31–35
                             Acts chapter 2 verses 14–21, 41–47
                             Joshua chapter 2 verses 1–21

Wherever I am I will   Psalm 40 verses 1–5
  praise you   Acts chapter 3 verses 1–11
  Lord   282   John chapter 7 verses 33–39

Prayers about the Holy Spirit

O Lord, When your Holy Spirit comes to live in us, you
begin to change our character so that we become more like
you. When we feel hatred towards someone, you can change
the hatred to love. You change sadness to joy, confusion
into peace, anger to patience, meanness to kindness and
naughtiness to goodness. It's good to know that we don't
have to stay the way we are, but can be changed by your
life in us. Thank you Lord,

                                            Amen.

Thank you, Heavenly Father, that when Jesus had gone back
from earth to heaven you sent the Holy Spirit to live in the
lives of those who believe in Jesus and have asked Him to
forgive their sins. Thank you that He lives in us to make us
more like Jesus, to teach more about Jesus, and to help us
tell others about Jesus. Thank you for his power in our lives,
changing us to be the people that you want us to be.

                              In Jesus' Name, Amen.

Heavenly Father, However much I want to be like Jesus and
behave well, I know that on my own I can never be good
enough. It's wonderful to know that you send your Holy
Spirit to live in us so that He can change us from inside and
give us your power to be different. Thank you that as your

Holy Spirit controls our behaviour we will become more like Jesus in the way we treat people, and His character will be seen in us. We ask that each day we might know the power of the Holy Spirit in our lives, helping us to live the Christian life.

In Jesus' Name, Amen.

Lord Jesus, When the Holy Spirit came upon the disciples at Pentecost, He gave them the ability to speak in different languages so that people from many countries could hear about you and put their trust in you. And then in the Book of Acts there are many times when you used the disciples to do miracles in people's lives so that they would believe that it was you who had sent the disciples and would turn to you to have their sins forgiven.

There are many people today who need to hear the gospel, and want to know that you are a powerful God, able to change their lives. We pray that you will use our lives however you want to, so that they may hear and believe. Help us to let you be God in our lives and through us reach others.

In your Name, Amen.

Heavenly Father, Thank you so much for the gift of your Holy Spirit to us. It's amazing to realise that when He comes to live within us, He brings your life to us, so we can have God living in us. That's exciting Lord: and that means that people should be able to tell that our lives as Christians are different to theirs. Sometimes though, we don't let you fill our whole lives and control the way we behave, and then we're no different to those who don't have you living within. Please help us to say 'no' to the selfish part of us that wants to go on living for ourselves, and hand over our whole lives to you for you to fill and control by your Holy Spirit.

For your glory, Amen.

Lord, Without your Holy Spirit in us, we are like lightbulbs that have been taken out of their sockets: we can't produce any light because we are not joined to the source of power. When the Holy Spirit comes to live within us, we are joined again to your life, and so your light can shine through us to those around.

Please forgive us for those things that we have done wrong today, and make us clean again so that your Holy Spirit can fill our lives and make us shine brightly with your power.

In Jesus' Name, Amen.

Dear God, I feel so awful when I've done something bad. I feel uncomfortable inside and unclean. I'd be ashamed if people were to see the way I feel sometimes.

You see me all the time don't you Lord: and it's your Holy Spirit who makes me feel *so* rotten when I've done something wrong, I have to stop and put it right. I'm glad that you do that or else I'd go on doing worse and worse things and getting further away from you.

Please don't ever let me stop knowing when I've done something wrong.

For Jesus' Sake, Amen.

Lord Jesus, Sometimes I feel so powerless: powerless against myself and the way I keep doing what I know is wrong: powerless against the evil things I see in the world around me: and powerless to help all those people who are in trouble and who need to know you. You sent your Holy Spirit to fill us with your power – a power much greater than me and my sin, much greater than the evil around and much greater than the needs of the people in trouble. Lord, help me to know your power in my life; I can't do anything on my own, but if I let you reign as Lord in my life, I know you can overcome all these things and work through me to help others.

Please do that.

In your Name, Amen.

Heavenly Father, There are some days when I feel as though I can't really be bothered to do very much, and some days when I feel as though I'm not any good at anything so there's no point trying.

I know that you don't like to see that attitude in me and that you have sent your Holy Spirit to encourage me when I feel like this, and to help me get on with the things I should be doing. Please teach me how to rely on His strength, and power so that you can work through me and use my life for your glory.

In Jesus' Name, Amen.

12 The Trinity

Father we adore you   44

Acts chapter 6 verses 9–15, chapter 7 verses 1–54
Psalm 95
John chapter 14 verses 21–26
John chapter 12 verses 1–8
Daniel chapter 3 verses 1–28

Father we love you   45

John chapter 12 verses 23–32
Psalm 86 verses 1–12
John chapter 16 verses 7–16

Praise God from whom all blessings flow   199

Psalm 67 verses 3–7
Psalm 145 verses 1–7
Psalm 100

Thank you God for sending Jesus 233

John chapter 14 verses 23–27
1 Peter chapter 1 verses 13–21
John chapter 3 verses 16–21
John chapter 16 verses 5–15

We really want to thank you Lord   268

1 Corinthians chapter 12 verses 12–27
Ephesians chapter 4 verses 4–16

Prayers about the Trinity

Dear God, Sometimes I get confused because I don't understand how you can be made up of three people, the Father, the Son, and the Holy Spirit, but I suppose we never will understand because you are God, and our minds aren't big enough to understand you completely. Please help us to understand as much as we need to, and allow the Holy Spirit to live within us and make us more like Jesus.

In His Name, Amen.

Lord God Almighty, We worship you today and bring you our praise. We worship you Heavenly Father, who created all things and who loved us so deeply that you sent your only son to die for us. We worship you Lord Jesus because you were willing to come and offer up your life for us on the cross, that we might be forgiven and made clean. We worship you Holy Spirit, because you come to live within us to give to us the life and power of God.

We praise you Father, Son and Holy Spirit, Amen.

O Lord, We know that from before the beginning of time you have been God. You alone have existed from before the foundation of this earth. You created the world and everything in it; by your power it is held together and you have given life to all men.

We praise and worship you that in your love you chose to create mankind, and then when we turned from you, you chose to buy us back to yourself by the death of your only son, the Lord Jesus. By your Holy Spirit you come to live within us once more that we might know and experience your life in us making us truly alive and remaking us into the people you intended us to be.

We don't understand why you should be so gracious to men, but we praise you and thank you for your love.

In Jesus' Name, Amen.

Lord God, Thank you for being our Heavenly Father to whom we belong, and by whom we are loved. Lord Jesus, thank you for being our Saviour, Lord, Brother and Friend. Holy Spirit, thank you that you have come to be our Comforter, Teacher, our Guide and our Strength.

Thank you God that in you we find all that we need:

Amen.

13   Bible Stories

A boy gave to Jesus five loaves and two fish   1

Luke chapter 9 verses 10–17
Mark chapter 6 verses 30–44

Barabbas was a bad man   18

Matthew chapter 27 verses 11–26
Mark chapter 15 verses 1–15
Luke chapter 23 verses 1–25

By blue Galilee   23

John chapter 4 verses 43–54
Mark chapter 4 verses 1–9
Luke chapter 4 verses 14–75

Children of Jerusalem   24

Luke chapter 2 verses 41–51
1 Samuel chapter 2 verse 26

Come listen to my tale   30

Jonah (extracts)

Come to Jesus, He's amazing   33

Mark chapter 10 verses 13–16
Luke chapter 18 verses 15–18

Daniel was a man of prayer   36

Daniel chapter 6 verses 1–24

Don't build your house on the sandy land   39

Psalm 27
Psalm 61
Matthew chapter 7 verses 2–29

How did Moses cross the Red Sea   83

Exodus chapter 14 verses 13–31

Hushed was the evening hymn   85

1 Samuel chapter 3 verses 1–19

Isaiah heard the voice of the Lord   114

Isaiah chapter 6 verses 1–13

Joshua fit the battle of Jericho   143

Joshua chapter 6 verses 1–20

Mister Noah built an   Genesis chapters 6 and 9
    ark   167

Oh the Lord looked   Genesis chapter 6 verse 9, chapter
    down   184   7 verse 5
                             Genesis verses 6–12

Only a boy called   1 Samuel chapter 17 verses 1–54
    David   190

Peter and James and   Luke chapter 5 verses 1–11
    John   197

Peter and John went to   Acts chapter 3 verses 1–11
    pray   198

Said Judas to   John chapter 12 verses 1–8
    Mary   211

The wise man built his   Matthew chapter 7 verses 24–29
    house upon the
    rock   252

Twelve men went to   Numbers chapter 13 verses 1–3,
    spy   261   17–33

We have a king who   Matthew chapter 21 verses 1–11
    rides on a   Luke chapter 19 verses 28–44
    donkey   264

When Israel was in   Extracts from Exodus chapters
    Egypt's land   276   5–13

Zaccheus was a very   Luke chapter 19 verses 1–10
    little man   300

Prayers on Bible Stories

A boy gave to Jesus five loaves and two fish

Lord Jesus, You took five loaves and two fish and used them to feed a crowd of five thousand people. And all that you did was to give thanks to your Father in heaven, and then break the food up amongst the people there so that everyone had enough. That's a miracle! Thank you that you can do the same miracle with *our lives* if we give them to you: you will take them and use them to help many people in different ways. Please take our lives and use them today.

Amen.

Lord Jesus, When you shared out that small meal among so many people, probably very few people knew whose food it was that you took. But you knew, and you were glad that someone was willing to give what they had for others. Please help us always to be willing to share what we have with others in need. Teach us not to boast about what we give but to be happy to know that you see our gifts and are pleased.

In your Name, Amen.

O Lord, In reading the story of the little boy who gave his food to you, it puts us to shame because we are often very selfish and do not want to give as we should. Thank you for working a miracle and for using that food, that the boy gave to you. Help us to understand that in giving you the things that we have, you can use them in ways we could never imagine – thank you Lord.

Amen.

Barabbas was a bad man

Dear Lord, I wonder how you felt when you knew that Barabbas had been released from the death sentence and you were to take his place. You were a good man, Barabbas was a bad man. It must have been terrible for you to have been sentenced to death without doing anything wrong. I thank you Lord that you didn't just take the place of Barabbas but you took the punishment for our sin as well. Help us never to forget that.

Amen.

O Lord God, Thank you for allowing Jesus to take the place of Barabbas. When Jesus was in the garden of Gethsemene there was a time when He asked *not* to take Barabbas' place. Thank you, however, that despite His fear Jesus wanted to do what *you* wanted Him to do, because He knew that by dying and rising again it provided a way for all people to get to know God. Thank you for all the pain and suffering you went through.

Amen.

Big man

Dear Jesus, It must have been a big decision for Peter to leave his life as fisherman to become your disciple. It would have meant leaving friends, family, home and money to travel with you, trusting you for everything he needed. Sometimes we say that we went to be your disciples and follow you, but then we find it hard to leave behind all our old ways and to obey you in everything.

Thank you that just as you changed Peter and made him a stronger disciple as time went by, so you can change us and make us more obedient and willing to follow you.

In your Name, Amen.

Lord, When you walked on the seashore you used to see many men working on their fishing nets and boats. Sometimes you would call them by name even though you had never met them before. Thank you that you knew each person by name and you wanted them to follow you. Help us to be like Simon Peter who was prepared to leave his fishing nets to follow you.

Amen.

By blue Galilee

Father, When Jesus walked beside Galilee He told the people of many amazing things. As I allow Jesus to be my teacher I pray that He will teach me many amazing things also.

Amen.

Father, It was many, many years ago when Jesus used to walk by Lake Galilee teaching the people. They didn't always recognise Him as their Saviour as many people still don't today. However, His teaching is also relevant today as it was then – help us to recognise this.

In His Name, Amen.

Children of Jerusalem

Dear Father, Whether we are young or old we can always pray to you, we can always sing to you and we can always read about you from the Bible. Help us to remember that we do not have to be in a church, or some place of worship to do these things, but we can pray to you whilst we are walking to school, we can sing to you when we are on our own and we can read about you whenever we like because the Bible is readily available. We pray for those in other countries who desperately need Bibles and food and ask that you will meet the many other needs they might have.

Thank you Lord, Amen.

O Lord, We pray today for our teachers and our mothers and fathers. We thank you for the opportunity of learning and we pray for all those who haven't got the same chances to learn as we do. Help us to appreciate all that our teachers and our parents do for us.

In your Name, Amen.

Come listen to my tale

Dear Lord, I like the story of Jonah, and the way he ran away from doing what you wanted. It shows me that not everyone in the Bible found it easy to follow you. Sometimes I feel like running away from doing what is right. Please help me to see as Jonah did in the end, that your ways are best, and that if we do as you ask us, our lives will be pleasing to you. Please help me to trust and obey you.

In Jesus' Name, Amen.

Heavenly Father, It was when Jonah was inside the big fish that he began to call out to you for help, and to realise that he should have obeyed what you had asked him to do. Sometimes we go through times that are hard, when life seems to go wrong. We want to be thankful for those times because often it is then that we take time to talk to you and listen to you; and when you can show us what direction you want us to go in.

Thank you that when we disobey you, you don't turn away from us, but help us to get back on your path.

Thank you, in Jesus' Name, Amen.

Come to Jesus, He's amazing

Lord Jesus, When we read the stories in the Bible of all that you did when you were on earth, we are amazed. You performed miracles that no-one else could do, you cared about people, and you taught them about God. Thank you that although we can't see you today, you are alive in heaven, and still able to do amazing things in our lives.

Amen.

Dear Lord Jesus, When you were alive on earth, people would bring their friends to you because you were such a wonderful person, and able to help others in so many ways. You have helped us by forgiving us for the things we have done wrong and by being our friend. Please let us be like those in the Bible; bringing our friends to you by telling them all about you and what you have done.

For your Sake, Amen.

Daniel was a man of prayer

Dear Lord, There are many Christians in some countries who are persecuted and put in prison if they are found praying to you, or teaching about you. We pray for them this morning that they will have the same strength and courage that Daniel had, and that they will continue to pray. We ask that, just as Daniel's praying led to many people finding you and putting their trust in you, so today those who persecute Christians may one day turn to you as their Saviour and Lord.

In Jesus' Name, Amen.

Dear Heavenly Father, Thank you for Daniel's willingness to pray despite what would happen if he was caught. Please forgive us that so often we are unwilling to pray just because we are lazy or cannot be bothered. Please help us to care enough about others so that we will be willing to pray for them. Thank you that it is a real privilege to be able to talk to you as our friend.

Amen.

Dear God, When we read the story of Daniel in the lions' den we are amazed at his bravery and the way he trusted you to look after him. He was able to trust you because he had spent so much time – praying and talking to you, and so he knew that you would look after him. Please teach us to pray at all times so that when difficult times come we will be able to trust you for your help.

In Jesus' Name, Amen.

Don't build your house on the sandy land

Dear Lord Jesus, Sometimes it seems that nothing is very certain in our lives; people we get to know move away, we are not sure what we will do when we leave school, sometimes even our families quarrel and that makes us unhappy. Thank you, though, that however insecure we may feel about what is going on around us, we know that you never change, and we can always be sure of your love and your care for us. Please help us to turn to you and allow you to fill us with your peace.

In your Name, Amen.

Dear Heavenly Father, It seems that people build their lives on different sets of rules; some people say that one thing is wrong when others say that it is right. How am I supposed to know what is right and how am I supposed to live my life? Thank you for the story that Jesus told about the two men building their houses on sand and rock. I want my life to be like the house built on the rock, that nothing can destroy. Jesus is described as a 'Rock' in the Bible – please help me to build my life upon Him, to obey Him and His teaching so that my life won't be shattered by storms that come along.

In Jesus' Name, Amen.

How did Moses cross the Red Sea?

Dear Heavenly Father, We praise you because you are such a powerful God. Thank you that nothing is impossible for you. You are the one who made the seas and the rivers and so for you it would be possible to make a path through the Red Sea for Moses and the Israelites to cross. Please help me to have faith in you like they did; to believe that when I am in trouble you can help me and show me the way through. Thank you that you understand my problems and want to help me in them. Thank you for loving me – in Jesus' name.

Amen.

Dear Lord, When Moses was leading the Israelites from Egypt into the promised land, they suddenly found themselves in trouble with the sea in front of them and the Egyptian army behind them. They probably thought that there was no way out and that they would all die, but when Moses prayed you showed that you had a plan to help them. Sometimes I feel a bit like that: I'm in trouble and there is no way out. Help me to remember that you always have a way of helping us if we will obey you and trust you.

In Jesus' Name, Amen.

Hushed was the evening hymn

Heavenly Father, It's wonderful to know that you chose to speak to a little boy like Samuel and tell him the things you were going to do and that you trusted him to listen to you and obey you. I'd like to be like Samuel; please teach me to listen to you as I pray and read the Bible so that I will recognise your voice and know the things you want to do in my life.

Amen.

Dear Lord, I think that if I had been Samuel I would have been a bit scared to know that you were talking to me. How did he know it was you speaking? Jesus said 'I am the Good Shepherd, a sheep will follow its shepherd because it knows his voice'. Thank you that as we get to know Jesus we get to know His voice and want to follow Him because we know He is good and will lead us in ways that are good. Please help us to know Him better.

In His Name, Amen.

Isaiah heard the voice of the Lord

Dear Heavenly Father, I want to be like Isaiah – ready to go wherever you want. When we hear stories about people who have spent their lives telling others about the Lord Jesus, it makes me want to go as well. I know that not all Christians have to go abroad to other countries; you want some to stay here. Please show me just where you want me to go. Even while I am still young please help me to tell others about your love and please make me ready for all that you have planned for my life.

For Jesus' sake, Amen.

Dear God, I think that if you wanted me to go and tell others about Jesus I would be quite scared because I might be laughed at and made fun of, and in some countries it can be dangerous to talk about you. When Isaiah offered to go and speak to others about you, you helped him by telling him what to say, and you gave him, your power to help him speak. Next time I have an opportunity to talk to someone about you, please remind me to ask you for your power and for the right words to say.

For Jesus' sake, Amen.

Dear Lord Jesus, Thank you for all those people who spend their lives telling others about you and the new life you have come to give to all men. We pray this morning especially for those missionaries whom we know (insert names) and ask that you will look after them and their families. Please help them in the work that they are doing and use them to bring many others to trust in you.

In your Name, Amen.

Joshua fit the battle of Jericho

Dear Father, Thank you for the story of Joshua. Thank you that it shows us what a great God you are and how you can do great things through us if we will let you. We know that Joshua won the battle of Jericho because he was obedient to what you had told him to do. We ask that you will help us to be obedient to the things you tell us to do as we read the Bible and allow you to speak to us through it.

In Jesus' Name, Amen.

Father, Before Joshua went to fight the battle of Jericho you promised him that you would be with him wherever he went so he did not have to be afraid. Thank you that you are with each one of us wherever we go so we don't have to be afraid either. Please help us whenever we feel afraid of doing something we know we should do, to remember that you are with us and to ask you for your help.

In Jesus' Name, Amen.

Mister Noah built an ark

Dear Heavenly Father, It must have been hard for Noah to build the ark as you told him to do, when everyone else was laughing at him and calling him a fool because they didn't believe that there was going to be a flood. Thank you for his obedience to you even though he was the only one. Whenever I find myself in a group of people who laugh at me for what I believe, please help me not to go along with the crowd but to do what is right. In the end you proved that Noah was right and you were pleased with him for trusting you; I want you to be pleased with my life; please help me to obey you.

In Jesus' Name, Amen.

Dear God, I love to see a rainbow in the sky. It reminds me that the sun can still shine even though it's raining. Thank you that in our lives when things seem dark and sad you can make the sun shine in our hearts because we know that you love us and care for us. Next time I see a rainbow please help me to remember that you love me.

Thank you, Lord. Amen.

Dear God, Thank you for saving the animals from the flood and putting them in the ark. Thank you for all the animals that you created; so many different kinds from the smallest insects to the big elephant. Thank you for our pets and the fun we can have with them. Please teach us how to look after animals and be kind to them.

Amen.

Thank you for Noah, Lord, and the way in which he did what you asked him. Noah's family and so many animals were saved from the flood because he trusted in you. Help us Lord to do whatever you ask of us and to have the same trust in you as Noah did. Then we can give you the glory.

In Jesus' precious Name, Amen.

Father, We thank you for this story of Noah and the flood. It is so difficult to imagine such a big flood and having to live in an ark for such a long time together with many animals. Noah trusted in you God and was saved. Help us Lord when difficulties face us to trust you.

In Jesus' Name, Amen.

Oh, the Lord looked down

Dear Heavenly Father, It must have seemed a crazy thing to Noah to be asked to build such an enormous ark and to be expected to believe that you would send enough water to make it float, and that anyone who wasn't in the ark would die in the flood. Sometimes I find it hard to believe that just as the ark was the only way of escaping the flood, so the only way that anyone can get to heaven is if they trust Jesus as their Saviour. Please help us to understand what it is for us to give our lives to Jesus so that as the people were saved who were in the ark, so we will be safe in Jesus.

In His Name, Amen.

Dear Lord Jesus, When the water started to fill the earth in the time of the flood, the people and animals in the ark must have felt safe, hidden away from the danger. Thank you that when difficult things happen in our lives, you can be like a hiding place and a shelter for us so that we don't get hurt by everything that is going on around us. Please help us to get to know you better so that we know who to come to when there are problems in our lives. Thank you for being a friend that we can turn to.

In your Name, Amen.

Only a boy called David

Dear Heavenly Father, Thank you that in the story of David killing Goliath you show that you can take our lives even when we are still young and use us in your work. All that was special about David was that he trusted in you and believed that you had the power to work through him. Thank you that when we trust you and remember that you are always with us. We have nothing to be afraid of because you can help us to be strong and full of courage.

Thank you Lord, Amen.

Dear Lord, When David offered to go and fight Goliath, people laughed at him and said that he was just a little boy and couldn't help. Sometimes I feel a bit like that; I seem so young and I don't think that I can do many things. But you used David to kill the giant everyone else was scared of. I'd like you to use my life if you want to: even though I don't feel very special, I want to give my life to you so that you can make it special. Thank you that you will do that because I ask in Jesus' Name.

Amen.

Peter and James and John

Dear Lord Jesus, So many times we try to do things the way that we want instead of the way that you want, and then often it all goes wrong and we end up in trouble. Please teach us that it is better to listen to what we are told to do, and to be obedient, than to go our own way. Help us to obey our Mummies and Daddies, and our teachers and all those people who are in authority like policemen and nurses.

In your Name, Amen.

Dear Lord Jesus, When the disciples did what you told them to do, you filled their nets with lots of fish so that their boats nearly sank because of the weight. Thank you that when we obey you, you fill our lives with many good things. Help us to obey you even when it is hard, because you only give us rules that are to make our lives happy and full of joy.

We ask it in your Name, Amen.

Peter and John went to pray

Dear Heavenly Father, Money seems to be so important in the world today. Some people don't have any, others have lots and lots, and for some people all they want to do with their lives is make money. When Jesus lived on earth He and his disciples never had much. Please help us to see that there are much more important things in life than having money. Instead of the disciples giving money to the lame beggar, they made him able to walk! Thank you for our health and our strong bodies to run around and enjoy life. Thank you for the gift of being able to know you.

In Jesus' Name, Amen.

Dear Lord Jesus, Thank you for your power to heal sick people. Thank you that you care about us when we are not feeling well. We want to pray today for people that we know who are ill (insert names). We ask that you will help them to know that you love them.

We ask it in Jesus' Name, Amen.

Said Judas to Mary

Dear Lord Jesus, What a beautiful thing Mary did, to bring her most valuable possession to you, for you to enjoy, and to show you how much she loved you. I want to tell you that I love you. I don't own anything very valuable, but I'd like to give you my life. Please make it into a life that is pleasing to you so that you can enjoy it.

For your sake I ask this, Amen.

Dear Lord Jesus, Sometimes I wonder how I can show you that I love you because I can't do anything like Mary did in the story. We can't bring perfume to you, but you say in the Bible, 'If you love me, you will do what I ask'. Even when I find it hard, please help me to do what you ask willingly and cheerfully as a way of telling you that I love you and am grateful to you for all that you have done for me.

Amen.

How sad, Heavenly Father, that Judas thought it was more important to sell Mary's ointment for money than to pour it out at Jesus' feet as a blessing to Him, Please teach us to have the right attitude to gifts and abilities that we have, so that we won't just want to use them to make money, but in order to bring glory and pleasure you you.

In Jesus' Name, Amen.

The wise man built his house upon the rock

Dear Heavenly Father, I'd like to grow up to be wise, not foolish. Thank you that being wise doesn't mean being very clever, and knowing lots of things, but learning to put into practise in my life all that I know about you and how you want me to live. That way my life will stand firm in storms like the wise man's house did, and that's what I want: please help me.

Amen.

Dear Lord Jesus, Thank you for the story of the two men building their houses on rock and on sandy land. Please help me to build my life on a rock; on you and your word, the Bible, even though sometimes I want to do things that I know are wrong. Help me to understand that while wrong things seem attractive at the time, they won't help our lives to be strong and firm, and when trouble comes we won't be able to stand up to it. Please make me strong in you, Lord Jesus,

Amen.

Twelve men went to spy

Dear God, When Moses sent some of the Israelites to explore Canaan, most of them came back frightened and only aware of the dangers that were in the country. But Joshua and Caleb saw all the good things that were there, and believd that you would help them to overcome all the dangers. Please help us to be like Joshua and Caleb and not turn our backs on something just because we are afraid to trust you. When we have to go to a new place like a new school or to hospital, help us to trust you to look after us.

Thank you God, Amen.

Dear Jesus, Please help us to be brave like Joshua and Caleb. Please help us to see all the good things in life that you give us and not be like the other ten men who only saw the bad things. Thank you for filling our lives with so much that is good, and for giving us the strength to overcome the problems in our lives.

Amen.

When Israel was in Egypt's land

Thank you Lord, for using Moses to free the people of Israel from Egypt. Even though he didn't think he could do anything, you used him to speak to Pharaoh and to lead the people out of slavery. Thank you that you can use our lives too, if we are willing to let you do what you want through us.

> In Jesus' Name, Amen.

What an amazing story, Lord, of the way you rescued the Israelites from being slaves in Egypt, and brought them out of that land into Canaan. Please help us to see that that is a picture of what happens when we become Christians. Thank you that you have the power to rescue us from Satan's kingdom of darkness and to bring us into your kingdom of light. Thank you also that when we become Christians our lives are no longer controlled by our selfish nature, but by your Holy Spirit, making us more like Jesus. Please make this change in us.

> In Jesus' Name, Amen.

Zaccheus was a very little man

Dear Lord Jesus, Sometimes we think that no-one ever notices us and the things we do, but you show us through Zaccheus that wherever we are, you see us and care about us. You knew his name without asking, and even in the middle of such a big crowd you took time to speak with him. Thank you Lord Jesus that you know each one of us by name and always have time to speak to us and to listen to us when we pray.

> Amen.

Lord Jesus, When you got to know people you didn't only have time for those who were good. You said that you had come to seek and to save those who were lost like Zaccheus who had been stealing money from people. Thank you so much that although you hate the bad things that we sometimes do, you still love us as people, and want to change us as you changed Zaccheus from doing wrong.

We are sorry for the wrong things that we have done even today, and pray that you will help us to put right what we can.

> In your Name, Amen.

14 The Bible and Scripture

Ask! Ask! Ask! and it
  shall be given
  you   11

Luke chapter 11 verses 5–13
Luke chapter 12 verses 22–34
Matthew chapter 7 verses 7–14

Be still and know   22

Psalm 46
Psalm 37 verses 1–11

Behold what manner of
  love   15

Galatians chapter 3 verse 26,
  chapter 4 verse 7
1 John chapter 3 verses 1–3
John chapter 1 verses 1–14
Romans chapter 8 verses 14–17

God so loved the
  world   59

John chapter 3 verses 16–21
1 John chapter 3 verses 16–24

He brought me to His
  banqueting
  house   73

Song Of Solomon chapter 2 verses
  1–4
Ephesians chapter 2 verses 1–10
Psalm 62

How lovely on the
  mountains   84

Isaiah chapter 52 verses 7–10
Revelation chapter 19 verses 4–7
Isaiah chapter 54 verses 1–14
Matthew chapter 28 verses 16–20

I am the way, the truth
  and the life   89

John chapter 14 verses 1–10
John chapter 11 verses 1–15, 21–27
1 John chapter 1 verse 1, chapter
  2 verse 2
Luke chapter 12 verses 16–21

I will make you fishers
  of men   123

Luke chapter 5 verses 1–11
Matthew chapter 4 verses 18–22
John chapter 1 verses 35–51
John chapter 21 verses 1–8

Jesus I will come with
  you   138

John chapter 14 verses 1–10
Luke chapter 14 verses 25–33
Matthew chapter 7 verses 13–20
John chapter 10 verses 11–18,
  27–30

Make the book live to me, O Lord 163

Luke chapter 24 verses 13–32
2 Timothy chapter 3 verses 14–17
John chapter 5 verses 39–47
Psalm 119 verses 1–18

Now be strong and very courageous 172

Joshua chapter 1 verses 1–9
1 John chapter 4 verses 11–18
Psalm 27
Isaiah chapter 41 verses 1–5

Search me, O God 212

Psalm 139
Psalm 51
1 John chapter 1 verse 5, chapter 2 verse 2

Seek ye first the kingdom of God 215

Luke chapter 12 verses 16–34
Matthew chapter 6 verses 25–34
Luke chapter 11 verses 5–13

Surely goodness and mercy 223

Psalm 23
Psalm 33
Lamentations chapter 3 verses 22–26

Tell me the old, old story 227

John chapter 3 verses 16–21
Colossians chapter 1 verses 9–23
Ephesians chapter 1 verses 3–14

Tell me the stories of Jesus 228

Luke chapter 10 verses 25–37
Luke chapter 15 verses 11–32
Matthew chapter 26 verses 36–46
Mark chapter 10 verses 13–16
Matthew chapter 28 verses 1–10

The best book to read is the Bible 234

Psalm 1
Psalm 119 verses 1–18
2 Timothy chapter 3 verses 14–17
Joshua chapter 1 verses 1–9

The joy of the Lord is my strength 240

Acts chapter 3 verses 1–8
Philippians chapter 4 verses 4–9
Nehemiah chapter 8 verses 1–12

The Lord's my   Psalm 23
  shepherd   243   John chapter 10 verses 1–21
                        Luke chapter 15 verses 1–7

Prayers about the Bible and Scripture

Thank you, Heavenly Father for the Bible and all the stories that it tells us. Please help us to spend more time reading the stories in the Bible so that we can find out more about you and the things that you have done. We pray for people who do not have a Bible because it is not allowed in their country or because it hasn't been put into their language yet. Please help all those who take Bibles to countries where they don't have them, and those who translate the Bible into different languages.

                        In Jesus' Name, Amen.

Father, We thank you for stories and for our imaginations which help us to enjoy lots of different kinds of stories; adventures, mysteries, romances, animal stories and stories about all different people. We thank you too for stories which are true; stories of people who really lived and of things that really happened. We know that the story of the Lord Jesus is true and we thank you that He really did come and live on this earth and then die for us. Thank you that all the stories in the Bible are true and that we can get to know more about you as we read them.

                        In Jesus' Name, Amen.

Thank you, Lord, that you have given us the Bible to help us get to know you: to tell us what your character is like, and how you have dealt with people throughout history, but most of all to show us the way that we can become your children by trusting in the Lord Jesus. Jesus said 'No man can come to me unless the Father draws him'. As we read the Bible, please open our eyes to what it teaches us about Jesus, and draw us close to Him.

                        We ask it in His Name, Amen.

Dear God, The Bible tells us that it is a book that you have inspired and written to tell us about yourself so that we can get to know you. It's amazing that you took ordinary people like farmers, doctors, fishermen and soldiers and used them to write the different books in the Bible. Thank you for their obedience to you that meant that you could use them to bring us your word. We pray that you will help us to tell other people the things that we have learnt from the Bible, so that your word will be spread through us to many more people.

In Jesus' Name, Amen.

Dear Lord, The Bible must be the most exciting book ever written: so many people were involved in writing the different parts of it, and it was written over thousands of years; yet all the books are linked together to tell the story of how you have been dealing with mankind since you created the world. It's wonderful to see how even in the Old Testament the writers told about the way Jesus would be born and then die for us. It's also wonderful to see how so many things that happened in the Old Testament are like pictures pointing to Jesus and all that He would do when He came. Thank you that the Bible isn't just like an ordinary history book, because it tells us *His Story*: the story of the Lord Jesus! Thank you for giving us the Bible.

In Jesus' Name, Amen.

Lord, In a world where there is so much confusion over what is right and what is wrong, it's good to know that we have the Bible, your Word, to tell us what your standards are, and to show us the way you want us to live. Even when people around us don't believe the Bible and won't live in the way it says, please help *us* to stick to it and keep your commandments.

In Jesus' Name, Amen.

Heavenly Father, Sometimes we find it hard to accept that you really do know what is best for our lives, and hard to live our lives within the boundaries you have given us in the Bible. But if we bought a car or a motorbike we would want to have an instruction book from the maker to show us how to look after the machine and to make it work to its fullest potential.

You made each one of us, and the Bible is like your instruction book for us to know how to live life to its fullest without spoiling or hurting ourselves. Please teach us to read the Bible more and to obey what you say to us through it.

In Jesus' Name, Amen.

Lord, When I find it hard to read the Bible and would rather be reading other books, help me to see how the Bible can be interesting and exciting. There are some good adventure stories in the Old Testament, and stories of peoples' lives that help us to see how we should live and what we shouldn't do. Then there are the Psalms – lots of songs of praise to you: help me to use them myself – to make them my songs and my way of praising you. Thank you for the gospels telling about the life of Jesus – showing me what a good and loving person He was, and also all the letters written to help churches and Christians know how they should live and work. I need to read it all if I want to learn to live as a Christian. And thank you for the parts of the Bible that tell us about the future, showing us that Jesus is coming again to earth, and helping us to have some idea of what heaven is like.

Please, Holy Spirit, make the Bible real to me and help me to live out the things that it shows me I should do. Most of all help me get to know Jesus better through reading it.

In His Name, Amen.

Father, Thank you for the Bible; thank you that it is more than just a book, it's your Word to us, your way of telling us about yourself. When we read the Bible it changes our lives, it's like a lamp that lightens the darkness of this world; a sword that which is good from that which is bad; a hammer breaking up the stoney hardness of our hearts, a seed that grows in our lives to produce fruit and flowers instead of weeds.

As we read your Word it encourages our faith and trust in you, and helps us to recognise the things in us that need to be changed. Thank you for the power of your Word.

In Jesus' Name, Amen.

15   Blessings and the Doxology

Lord dismiss us with
  your blessing   155

Isaiah chapter 40 verses 28–31
John chapter 14 verses 1–26
Galatians chapter 5 verses 16–26

Praise God from whom
  all blessings
  flow   199

Psalm 67
Psalm 145
Revelation chapter 4 verses 1–11
Exodus chapter 16 verses 1–36

Shalom my friend   217

John chapter 14 verses 23–31
Psalm 29
Isaiah chapter 25 verses 3–12

Lord we ask now to
  receive your
  blessing   301

Numbers chapter 6 verses 24–26
1 Corinthians chapter 13 verses
  1–8
John chapter 17 verses 11–13

Blessings and the Doxology

May the Lord bless you and take care of you;
May the Lord be kind and gracious to you;
May the Lord look on you with favour,
and give you peace.

                Numbers chapter 6 verses 24–26

Praise the Lord, the God of Israel
He alone does wonderful things.
Praise His glorious name forever.
May His glory fill the whole world.
Amen, Amen.

                Psalm 72 verses 18–29

The Lord will guard you;
He is by your side to protect you.
The sun will not hurt you during the day,
nor the moon during the night.

The Lord will protect you from all danger;
He will keep you safe.
He will protect you as you come and go
Now and forever.

Psalm 121 verses 5–8

The grace of the Lord Jesus Christ, the love of God, and the fellowship of the Holy Spirit be with you all.

2 Corinthians chapter 13 verse 14

To Him who by means of His power working in us is able to do so much more than we can ever ask for, or even think of: to God be the glory in the church and in Christ Jesus for all time, for ever and ever. Amen.

Ephesians chapter 3 verses 20–21

To the eternal King, immortal and invisible, the only God – to Him be honour and glory for ever and ever. Amen.

1 Timothy chapter 1 verse 17

May the God of peace provide you with every good thing you need in order to do His will, and may He, through Jesus Christ, do in us what pleases Him. And to Christ be the glory for ever and ever. Amen.

Hebrews chapter 13 verses 20–21

To Him who is able to keep you from falling, and to bring you faultless and joyful before His glorious presence – to the only God our Saviour through Jesus Christ our Lord, be glory, majesty, might, and authority, from all ages past, and now, and for ever and ever. Amen.

Jude verses 24–25

Unto Him that loves us, and by His sacrificial death has freed us from our sins and made us a kingdom of priests to serve His Food and Father. To Jesus Christ be the glory and power for ever and ever, Amen.

Revelation chapter 1 verses 5–6

To Him who sits upon the throne and to the Lamb,
be praise and honour, glory and might,
for ever and ever.

Revelation chapter 5 verse 13

Praise, glory, wisdom, thanksgiving, honour, power and might belong to our God for ever and ever. Amen.

Revelation chapter 7 verse 12

16   Christian Living

Abba Father   2

Romans chapter 8 verses 14–17
Luke chapter 16 verses 1–13
Revelation chapter 2 verses 1–7
Mark chapter 14 verses 32–42
Matthew chapter 6 verses 5–15

Be bold   14

Exodus chapters 3 and 4
Joshua chapter 1 verses 6–9
Deuteronomy chapter 31 verses 1–8
1 John chapter 4 verses 11–18
1 Samuel chapter 17 verses 1–58

Bind us together
  Lord   17

1 Corinthians chapter 12 verses 12–27
Ephesians chapter 4 verses 2–6
John chapter 17 verses 6–12, 20–23

Come on, let's get up
  and go   31

Romans chapter 10 verses 13–17
John chapter 4 verses 1–42
Psalm 100
Isaiah chapter 35 verses 1–10

Don't build your house
  on the sandy
  land   39

Psalm 27
Psalm 61
Matthew chapter 1 verses 24–29

Do you want a
  Pilot?   40

Luke chapter 8 verses 22–25
Ecclesiastes chapter 11 verse 9,
  chapter 12 verse 7
John chapter 10 verses 1–14, 27–30

Give me oil in my
  lamp   50

Matthew chapter 25 verses 1–13
Zechariah chapter 1 verses 1–14
John chapter 14 verses 15–26

God forgave my
  sin   54

Psalm 32
Matthew chapter 6 verses 9–15
Ephesians chapter 4 verses 17–32
Matthew chapter 10 verses 1–15
Luke chapter 21 verses 1–4

God whose Son   62

Acts chapter 2
1 Corinthians chapter 12 verses 1–11

He who would valiant be   80

Luke chapter 14 verses 25–33
Numbers chapter 13 verses 1–3, 17–33
Ephesians chapter 6 verses 10–18
1 Samuel chapter 17 verses 1–58

I am trusting you Lord Jesus   86

John chapter 14 verses 1–6, 15–21
Psalm 25
Proverbs chapter 3 verses 1–7
Luke chapter 8 verses 41–56

I can run through a troop   90

Psalm 18 verses 1–3, 25–33
Psalm 62
Romans chapter 7 verse 14, chapter 8 verse 4

I do not know what lies ahead   92

Matthew chapter 6 verses 25–34
Psalm 48
Isaiah chapter 58 verses 8–14

If you see someone   95

Luke chapter 10 verses 30–37
Matthew chapter 25 verse 31–46

I have decided to follow Jesus   98

Luke chapter 9 verses 52–62
1 John chapter 2 verses 15–17
Luke chapter 14 verses 25–33
Luke chapter 5 verses 27–32

In our work and in our play   108

Luke chapter 2 verses 41–52
Galatians chapter 5 verses 16–26
Mark chapter 10 verses 13–16

It's a happy day   118

2 Peter chapter 1 verses 3–8
Psalm 77
Psalm 1

I've got peace like a river   120

John chapter 14 verses 23–27
Colossians chapter 3 verses 12–17
Galatians chapter 5 verses 16–26

I've got that joy, joy,
  joy, joy 121

Psalm 16
Isaiah chapter 35 verses 1–10
John chapter 15 verses 1–17

I want to live for Jesus
  everyday 122

Luke chapter 12 verses 16–21
Luke chapter 18 verses 18–27
Mark chapter 8 verses 34–38

I want to walk with
  Jesus Christ 124

Luke chapter 14 verses 25–33
1 John chapter 1 verses 5–10
Philippians chapter 2 verses 5–16

Just as I am, your child
  to be 146

Luke chapter 14 verses 15–24
Matthew chapter 11 verses 25–30
Luke chapter 15 verses 11–32
1 Samuel verses 1–19

Keep me shining
  Lord 147

Matthew chapter 5 verses 13–16
Luke chapter 8 verses 22–25
Zechariah chapter 1 verses 1–14

Make me a channel of
  your peace 161

Psalm 37 verses 1–11
Matthew chapter 5 verses 1–16
2 Corinthians chapter 1 verses 2–7
Matthew chapter 6 verses 9–15
Mark chapter 8 verses 34–38

Make me a
  servant 162

Matthew chapter 20 verses 20–28
Luke chapter 22 verses 14–27
John chapter 13 verses 1–16
Acts chapter 20 verses 28–35

May the mind of Christ
  my Saviour 165

Philippians chapter 2 verses 1–11
Psalm 1
Psalm 119 verses 1–16
John chapter 14 verses 23–28

My faith is like a staff
  of oak 168

Hebrews chapter 10 verse 38,
    chapter 11 verse 6
Luke chapter 7 verses 1–10
Ephesians chapter 6 verses 10–20

Now be strong and
  very
  courageous   172

Joshua chapter 1 verses 1–9
1 John chapter 4 verses 11–18
Psalm 27
Isaiah chapter 41 verses 1–5
Exodus chapters 3 and 4

One more step along
  the world I go   188

Psalm 48
John chapter 10 verses 11–18,
  27–30
Romans chapter 12 verses 1–2
Philippians chapter 4 verses 4–9

Peace I give to
  you   196

John chapter 14 verses 23–31
John chapter 7 verses 37–39
1 Corinthians chapter 13 verses
  1–8

Put your hand in the
  hand   206

Matthew chapter 8 verses 23–27
Luke chapter 5 verses 1–11
John chapter 2 verses 13–17

Spirit of the living
  God   222

Acts chapter 2
Acts chapter 19 verses 1–6
John chapter 14 verses 15–26
Psalm 51

Stand up, stand up for
  Jesus   226

Ephesians chapter 6 verses 10–30
2 Timothy chapter 2 verses 1–10
1 Corinthians chapter 9 verses
  24–27
Romans chapter 8 verses 35–39

The greatest thing in all
  my life   239

Philippians chapter 1 verses 21–30
Luke chapter 2 verses 41–52
1 Corinthians chapter 9 verses
  19–23

The joy of the Lord is
  my strength   240

Acts chapter 3 verses 1–8
Philippians chapter 4 verses 4–9
Nehemiah chapter 8 verses 1–12

The Lord has need of me   242

Matthew chapter 25 verses 14–30
2 Timothy chapter 2 verses 1–10
2 Timothy chapter 4 verses 1–8
1 Samuel chapter 3 verses 1–19

The Lord is my shepherd   244

Psalm 23
John chapter 10 verses 1–21
Luke chapter 15 verses 1–7

There's new life in Jesus   249

1 John chapter 5 verses 1, 9–13
Psalm 32
Matthew chapter 9 verses 18–26
John chapter 11 verses 1–44

The wise man built his house upon the rock   252

Psalm 27
Psalm 61
Matthew chapter 7 verses 24–29

The wise may bring their learning   253

Matthew chapter 2 verses 1–12
Psalm 50 verses 1–3, 23
Psalm 92 verses 1–5
Hebrews chapter 13 verses 15–16

Though the world has forsaken God   257

Matthew chapter 7 verses 13–20
John chapter 13 verses 31–35
Acts chapter 2 verses 14–21, 41–47
Joshua chapter 2 verses 1–21

This little light of mine   258

Matthew chapter 5 verses 13–16
1 John chapter 1 verses 5–10
Isaiah chapter 60 verses 1–3, 19–22
John chapter 1 verses 1–13

Turn your eyes upon Jesus   260

Colossians chapter 3 verses 1–17
Luke chapter 9 verses 27–36
Revelation chapter 1 verses 9–18

When I needed a neighbour   275

Matthew chapter 25 verses 31–46
Luke chapter 10 verses 30–37

When the road is rough
  and steep   279

Isaiah chapter 42 verses 1–2
Matthew chapter 14 verses 22–33
Matthew chapter 28 verses 16–20
Daniel chapter 3 verses 1–28

Wherever I am I'll
  praise Him   282

Psalm 34 verses 1–10
Psalm 63
Acts chapter 3 verses 1–11

Wherever I am I will
  praise you
  Lord   283

Psalm 40 verses 1–5
Acts chapter 3 verses 1–11
John chapter 7 verses 33–39

Who is on the Lord's
  side?   287

Matthew chapter 12 verses 24–37
1 Samuel chapter 17 verses 1–51
Psalm 98
2 Timothy chapter 2 verses 1–10

Will your anchor
  hold?   290

Psalm 62
Matthew chapter 8 verses 23–27
Mark chapter 6 verses 45–52

Your ways are
  higher   295

John chapter 14 verses 1–6
Isaiah chapter 55 verses 1–13
Romans chapter 11 verses 33–36

Prayers about Christian Living

Thank you Lord Jesus that you know everythimg about us because you are always with us. Please help us to live our lives for you so that you will be pleased with them and so that other people might come to know you because of us. Teach us not to be selfish but always willing to help others.

In Jesus' Name, Amen.

Dear Lord, It's so wonderful to know that when you forgive our sins, you also forget them. We're not like that if one of our friends hurts us: we usually keep reminding them of what they have done and try to make them feel bad about it. Please teach us to forgive others as you forgive us, not holding things against people, but putting whatever it was behind and forgetting it. Help us to do this even when someone has hurt us very badly.

For Jesus' sake, Amen.

Lord Jesus, Thank you that being a Christian doesn't mean just having to obey a whole set of rules about what we should and shouldn't do, because you know that we could never do all the right things all the time. Thank you that instead, being a Christian means knowing you; knowing your forgiveness for the things we have done wrong or not done that we should have done, but also knowing you as a Person, as our Friend. Although we cannot see you we know that you are alive, and that we can talk to you in prayer, and get to know you better through reading the Bible. Thank you that as we spend time with you, you will give us your power within us to live as you want us to. Please help us to take the time to get to know you better than we do.

In your Name, Amen.

I feel like something good is going to happen God:
either to me, which would be great,
or to someone who is precious to me,
and that'd be great as well.

Even if nothing out-of-the-ordinary happens
I just want to say 'Thank you'
for the ordinary,
for just being alive,
and for this feeling of excitement
It's good!
Thank you.

Jesus, I feel great,
just great!
I may not feel like this tomorrow,
but I just wanted to let you know
that I'm glad I feel great today.
Thank you, Jesus.

Dear Lord, Place within our mouths praise to you, place within our minds purity from you, place within our hearts love for you.

We ask this in your Name, Amen.

Dear Lord, You promised us in the Bible that if we put our trust in you, you will never leave us alone and in spite of all the wrong things we do you will never disown us. Thank you Lord that each person is important to you and that you want so best for each one of us – help us not to abuse that,

Amen.

Dear God, I used to think it would be boring to be a Christian. I thought that obeying you meant giving up all the things that I enjoy doing and not having any fun any more. But now, when I read the stories of people in the Bible, and other Christians who have lived through history, I see that their lives really were exciting and full. Jesus said 'I have come so that you might have life to the full'; that's the kind of life I want, no please help me to live my life the Jesus way.

In His Name, Amen.

God,
is it true
that boredom is a belly-rumble of a hungry mind?
If so, then my mind isn't rumbling,
it's erupting!
I'm bored, really, really bored.
They say we're in for even more unemployment,
more leisure time,
so it's going to get worse, this boredom.
I do things when I'm bored
that I'm sorry for later on;
I make others feel miserable as well.
Please help me to learn
how to care for and feed my mind,
how to keep it completely satisfied
Will you?

I feel as if nothing could move me;
as if my roots went down a million miles
through solid rock;
as if I could withstand anything.

Is it stupid or dangerous to feel as secure as this?
Is it asking for trouble?
What if it is.
What if the worst happened.
I know where my roots are –
in you. Lord!
I trust you.
But the problem
is that I become self-confident,
and then, ask for it or not,
I get trouble,
and my security evaporates

If I keep on trusting in you,
nothing can move me.
Thank you, Lord
for being such a sure foundation.

Father, You are so dependable and there is nothing in our
lives that you don't know or care about. Lord, we love to
spend time with you, praising you, listening to you, walking
with you – knowing that you also want to spend time with
us. We want to become more like you – help us Lord to do
this.

Amen.

O, God, We thank you that you have given us our hearts,
our hands and our voices to praise you. We thank you that
you give us many gifts which are so often forgotten. You
have given us the gift of love, but we seem to spoil it. You
have given us the gift of peace but we seem to ignore it. You
have given us the gift of hope but we never seem to accept
it. O Lord teach us day by day to look after the gifts that you
have given us.

Amen.

I sense a craving in the world, Jesus,
a hunger for peace.
I share this feeling.
It makes me want to march, sometimes,
to join one of the peace movements,
but then I hesitate and I don't know why.

I feel strongly about it:
there ought not to be wars;
it's wrong for more to be spent on weapons
than on medical research;
those with power do seem to abuse it,
more often than not;
am I wrong?
I don't mean to be critical of others,
there's aggression and selfishness in me.
Forgive me, Lord.

I cannot imagine how someone as insignificant as me
could ever influence anyone towards peace,
but if, with your help, such a thing is possible,
help me, Lord,
help me.
I'd like to be a peacemaker.

I've heard people talk about things
getting worse –
wars, the weather, the whole world –
but I actually feel hopeful

Maybe it's because it is a fact that
light always chases darkness away:
by the sun's rising,
by a candle's gleaming,
by the flick of a switch,
and without fail when there is power.
Lord, you *are* power,
you are light;
the Light of the world;
and you never fail.
You give me hope.
Thank you.

O God our Heavenly Father, Help me in all that I do today not to cause anger or irritation in anyone. Help me to follow the example of Christ and love the people I find difficult to get on with. This seems to be impossible but with your help you can make it possible. Help me to believe that.

Amen.

Dear Lord, Whenever I watch the news on television, it seems to be bad news: There are so many wars going on, and people being killed, or there is trouble because people want more money and are on strike. Sometimes at the end of the news they tell us something good that has happened that day to cheer us up or make us laugh. I like to hear good news. Thank you that that's what the word 'gospel' means: good news, telling us that even though there are bad things happening in the world, God is still in control of the world and that if we let Him, He will live in our lives, and through us bring peace in the world. Thank you that we can say 'Our God reigns'.

In Jesus' Name, Amen.

It is good Lord, to know that you are king of the whole world – more than that, the whole universe. Sometimes when we look around there seems to be chaos everywhere, people are at war, nations are oppressed, families argue and lots of people don't have any jobs. We know that these problems are not your falt Lord. We know that if everyone allowed you to reign in their hearts then there would be peace on earth. Forgive us when we try to be king in our own lives and help us to let you reign so that we can start being peacemakers.

In Jesus' Name. Amen.

Thank you Heavenly Father that you are good. Thank you that everything you make and do is good. There is so much badness in the world it can be very confusing. But thank you that you care for us and only want good things for our lives.

We pray for those who don't know what you are like, who might even be frightened of you. We pray that they will look at Jesus and see just how good his life was on earth. Thank you that he can take away our sin and set us free from badness, so we can live a life full of goodness day by day.

In Jesus' Name, Amen.

Dear Lord Jesus, The Bible tells us that as Christians, we are like soldiers fighting a battle against Satan and his kingdom of darkness. Thank you that you are the leader of our army; our captain. Please teach us to obey you as ordinary soldiers would obey their captain, so that together we can be a strong army. Thank you that in your army we know that we have the victory because when you died and then rose to life again you defeated Satan and destroyed his power. Thank you that in your name we have the victory over all that is evil and against you. Help us to fight as your soldiers so that Satan's kingdom gets less and less, and yours spreads on earth.

In Jesus' Name we pray, Amen.

Lord Jesus, your Name is very special. Angels love it, demons fear it and men for hundreds of years have worshipped it. We know that in your Name we are conquerors over death, evil, darkness and madness. There are many battles going on in the world within people and between people and the true victory of peace can only be found in you.

Thank you that in our weakness you are strong. Help us not to fight our battles and tackle our problems in our own strength, but to hand them over to you and to accept whatever happens.

In your Name, Amen.

Heavenly Father, In the Bible we read that you have created angels and other creatures that we cannot see and that they are fighting a battle because some of them have turned against you and are trying to stop your work. Thank you that we know that those on your side will win that battle and destroy those who are against you. Thank you for the angels who look after us and fight for us as they fought for Elisha. Thank you for all the ways you look after us and show your love to us.

In Jesus' Name, Amen.

Dear Father, We pray that you will teach us to become soldiers for you: part of your army that is fighting here on earth for your kingdom. Thank you that Jesus is our king and the leader of our army. Please help us to obey Him and follow Him closely.

In His Name, Amen.

Lord Jesus, You know the many battles we have in our lives: battles against selfishness, anger, disobedience, bad thoughts, and many other things that are wrong in our lives. They seem such difficult battles: whenever I really make an effort to do what is right, it seems that I usually fail, and end up doing what I know is wrong. Please forgive me for the many times I have hurt you and other people by doing the wrong thing, and please teach me how to say 'No' to my old way of living, and allow your Holy Spirit to live your life through me instead.

Thank you that through your power we can be changed and can start to live the way you want us to.

Thank you in Jesus' Name, Amen.

You know what I'm scared of, don't you Jesus?
I try to pretend I'm brave,
but you know better
So do I.
Why am I scared of being scared?

I heard somewhere that fear is good, it's necessary:
if we couldn't feel fear we'd make all sorts
of terrible mistakes;
but still, I don't feel glad or grateful
when my fears come –
I just feel all tight inside.

Perhaps, Jesus, if you helped me
to look forward to good things
instead of being afraid of the bad
maybe then I would feel better
Does that make sense?

It wasn't as bad as I thought it would be.
I worried for nothing, didn't I?
I feel so relieved.
Thank you, Lord.

Am I too much of a pessimist?
Whatever . . .
I feel good now.

Sure, it wasn't a barrel of laughs,
but it was nowhere near as bad as I'd feared.
I'm sure there must be something to learn,
something about trusting you.
Be my teacher, Lord.

Thank you Lord Jesus for the story of how you made a storm calm when you were in the boat with the disciples, and how you brought them safely to the other side of the lake. Thank you that when we ask you to come into our lives you will guide us as you guided the boat and you will bring peace and calm into our lives even when we are having problems.

In your Name, Amen.

Lord Jesus, You said to your disciples 'My peace I give to you'. If there is anything the world needs now it is peace. Sometimes that seems impossible, but with you and only you we can have peace with God and then peace with those around us.

It is helpful to think of your peace as being like a river. It is strong, fresh, life-giving and always flowing towards the rest of the world – the sea. People can sit by it and be comforted. They can fish from it and be fed or they can drink from it and have their thirst quenched. As long as the source is clean and pure, as long as it is you then others will see your peace in us. We pray we won't clutter it up with the debris of unforgiven sin.

In your Name, Amen.

Dear Lord Jesus, Heaven must be such a wonderful place; no-one sad or crying, no sickness, or pain, and no death. And because You reign as king in heaven, there will be no fighting or wars, only peace and love between people. Thank you that one day we will see you in heaven: we will see your brightness and beauty, and we will be able to join in with the angels singing your praise and worshipping you. We are so looking forward to that time; please teach us how to trust you while we here on earth and allow you to reign in our lives as king, so that we may know that one day we will come to be with you in heaven.

In your Name, Amen.

Dear Lord Jesus, Thank you that every day is a new beginning. I don't need to look back, but I can look forward to new opportunities and adventures. Thank you for every smile, every friend who shows real love. Thank you for teaching me many important things today. Thank you, that you still love me although I sometimes fail.

Because you know all about me I want to begin this day with you Lord.

Amen.

It makes such a difference Lord, when someone says 'thank you'. It means that they have seen what I have done and appreciated it: it makes me feel good to know that I've done something well and helped others. Please remind me to say 'thank you' to those who help me, and most of all, to you, who gave your whole life for me.

Thank you Lord, Amen.

It's so easy to complain Lord, to grumble about the people I don't like, the things I don't have, the work I must do. Help me to stop complaining and to start being thankful for all that I have.

In Jesus' Name, Amen.

Dear God, We often think that the most important needs in life are material things like the clothes we wear and the food we eat, and we spend a lot of time thinking about these things. Please help us to understand that it is far more important to think about you and what you want to do in our lives than to think about material things. Thank you that when we do put you first in all that we do, we find that you supply everything we need anyway.

Thank you Lord, Amen.

17 Church

All over the world   5

Isaiah chapter 11 verses 1–9
Joel chapter 2 verses 23–32

Bind us together
    Lord   17

1 Corinthians chapter 12 verses
    12–27
Ephesians chapter 4 verses 2–6
John chapter 17 verses 6–12, 20–23
1 John chapter 2 verses 7–11,
    chapter 4 verses 7–12

Brothers and
    sisters   21

Galatians chapter 3 verse 26,
    chapter 4 verse 7
Ephesians chapter 4 verses 1–16
Psalm 133

For I'm building a
    people of power   47

Ephesians chapter 2 verses 11–22
Psalm 149
John chapter 17 verses 1, 13–23
Matthew chapter 16 verses 13–20

God is working his
    purpose out   57

Isaiah chapter 11 verses 1–10
Isaiah chapter 55 verses 6–11
1 Thessalonians chapter 4 verse
    13, chapter 5 verse 11

I hear the sound of the
    army of the
    Lord   100

2 Kings chapter 6 verses 8–17
2 Timothy chapter 2 verses 1–10
Ephesians chapter 6 verses 10–18
Ezekiel chapter 37 verses 1–14

I may never march in
    the infantry   101

1 Samuel chapter 17 verses 1–51
Psalm 98
2 Timothy chapter 2 verses 1–10

I sing a song of the
    saints   115

Psalm 145 verses 1–13
Hebrews chapter 11–12 verse 1
2 Corinthians chapter 6 verses
    1–10

O when the saints 195	Revelation chapter 4 verses 1–11 Revelation chapter 20 verses 11–15 and chapter 21 verses 1–5 Revelation chapter 19 verses 1–9 Philippians chapter 2 verses 5–11
Stand up, stand up for Jesus 226	Ephesians chapter 6 verses 10–20 2 Timothy chapter 2 verses 1–10 1 Corinthians chapter 9 verses 24–27 Romans chapter 8 verses 35–39
We really want to thank you Lord 268	1 Corinthians chapter 12 verses 12–27 Ephesians chapter 4 verses 4–16
Your hand O God has guided 298	Ephesians chapter 4 verses 1–6 Matthew chapter 22 verses 1–14 Exodus 13 verses 18–22 and chapter 14 verses 1–31 Psalm 145

Prayers for the Church (see also

Prayers for Pentecost)

Dear Lord Jesus, We thank you for the life you lived here on earth and for the way your whole life was spent for others: healing them and teaching them about God and how to put their lives right with Him and with each other. We know that you want to use us now to be your body on earth, to do the things you used to do, and we pray that you will find us with your Holy Spirit so that we may have your power to live as your body, so that others may see you working through us, and come to know you.

In your Name we pray, Amen.

Father, We know that as Christians you want us to serve other people and to show them your love. Thank you that you don't ask us to do that alone but to work together as your body, each one of us having a special job to do like the different parts of our bodies have different jobs. Please help us to know what the job is that you want each of us to do, and help us to remember that each person's job is equally important in showing your love to the world.

In Jesus' Name, Amen.

Dear Heavenly Father, We know that throughout history men and women have been punished and even killed because they believed in you and lived their lives for you. In many countries today people are put in prison or badly treated because of their faith. We pray for those people today, and ask that they might be aware of your love and presence in their lives today. Please help them to keep on standing up for what they believe even when it is hard for them, and to love those who are ill-treating them.

In Jesus' Name, Amen.

Heavenly Father, Today we pray especially for those who are the leaders of our church. We pray that you will give them wisdom to know how to direct your work here in the church, and how to help all the people whom they meet in their work. We pray for those who teach us in Sunday school, thank you for them, and ask you to help them to teach us more about you.

In Jesus' Name, Amen.

Dear Father, When we look at the church today, it's hard to understand why there are so many divisions and arguments among Christians. Jesus said that by the love we Christians have for one another, others would know that we belong to Him, but sometimes all that other people see is that we don't get on very well. Please forgive us for the times we have had arguments with other Christians and not put it right. Help us to live at peace with each other and show others that we can be united by your love.

For Jesus' Sake, Amen.

Dear Lord Jesus, It's amazing to realise that throughout the world there are millions of Christians, and that though they are all so different in many ways, they are all part of the same body: your body here on earth. As we learn to live our lives together and share what we have with each other, more people will see Jesus' love in us and know that we are His disciples. Please use our lives as an example to others of your love.

We ask it in Jesus' Name, Amen.

Thank you dear heavenly Father, for making us part of your family. It is good to know that we belong to you, and to each other as brothers and sisters. Please teach us to love one another however different it may seem, and to care for those who are in your family and live in countries where they have very little to eat and maybe nowhere to live. Help us to share things with them as we would with our own family.

For Jesus' Sake, Amen.

Since first I asked your forgiveness, Lord,
and since I asked you to come into my life,
I have a deep-down sense of belonging.
I feel accepted;
accepted by you.
Yes, by you, and that's great!

I also feel accepted by other people,
the rest of your family,
and that's great too.
Thank you for all my new brothers and sisters.

Being accepted into your family,
by you and them,
is going to make a big difference in my life.
Thank you.

Dear Father, We want to thank you so much for the life that you have given to us. Thank you for bringing us to know your love and for making us part of your family. Thank you that because we all belong to you, we belong to each other; it's so good to know that we have so many people who love us and whom we can love. Sometimes we don't feel very special or important but please help us to remember always that each of us *is* important to you and help us to show special love to those who are lonely and unloved.

In Jesus' Name, Amen.

18   Commitment

Abba Father 2

Romans chapter 8 verses 14–17
Mark chapter 14 verses 32–42
Matthew chapter 6 verses 5–15
Genesis chapter 11 verse 28, chapter 12 verse 9
Genesis chapter 22 verses 1–17

Blessed assurance 20

1 John chapter 1 verse 5, chapter 2 verse 2
Colossians chapter 3 verses 1–17
John chapter 3 verses 1–17

Do you want a Pilot? 40

Luke chapter 8 verses 22–25
Ecclesiastes chapter 11 verse 9, chapter 12 verse 7

Father, I place into your hands 42

Psalm 25
Psalm 139
Deuteronomy chapter 33 verses 26–29
Matthew chapter 6 verses 25–34

Father, lead me day by day 43

Luke chapter 4 verses 1–14
Mark chapter 1 verses 9–13
Exodus chapter 14 verses 1–31

Father we adore you 44

Psalm 95
John chapter 14 verses 21–26
John chapter 12 verses 1–8
Daniel chapter 3 verses 1–28
Acts chapter 6 verses 9–15, chapter 7 verses 1–54

I am trusting you Lord Jesus 86

John chapter 14 verses 1–6, 15–21
Psalm 25
Proverbs chapter 3 verses 1–7
Luke chapter 8 verses 41–56

I have decided to
  follow Jesus 98

Luke chapter 9 verses 57–62
1 John chapter 2 verses 15–17
Luke chapter 14 verses 25–33
Luke chapter 5 verses 27–32

I met Jesus at the
  crossroads 102

Matthew chapter 7 verses 13–20
Joshua chapter 24 verses 14–28
Luke chapter 12 verses 16–31
Matthew chapter 19 verses 16–30

I met you at the
  cross 103

John chapter 19 verses 25–30
Luke chapter 23 verses 33–43

I want to live for Jesus
  every day 122

Luke chapter 12 verses 16–21
Luke chapter 18 verses 18–27
Matthew chapter 8 verses 34–38

I want to walk with
  Jesus Christ 124

Luke chapter 14 verses 25–33
1 John chapter 1 verses 5–10
Philippians chapter 2 verses 5–16

Jesus is knocking,
  patiently
  waiting 135

Revelation chapter 3 verses 20
Matthew chapter 7 verses 7–12
John chapter 10 verses 7–18

Jesus I will come with
  you 138

John chapter 13 verse 36, chapter
  14 verse 6
Luke chapter 5 verses 1–11
Luke chapter 5 verses 27–32

Just as I am, your child
  to be 146

Luke chapter 14 verses 15–24
Matthew chapter 11 verses 25–30
Luke chapter 15 verses 11–32
1 Samuel chapter 3 verses 1–18

Put your hand in the
  hand 206

Matthew chapter 8 verses 23–27
Luke chapter 5 verses 1–11
John chapter 2 verses 13–17

Spirit of the living
  God 222

Acts chapter 2
Acts chapter 19 verses 1–6
John chapter 14 verses 15–26
Psalm 51

The Lord has need of
  me   242

Matthew chapter 25 verses 14–30
2 Timothy chapter 2 verses 1–10
2 Timothy chapter 4 verses 1–8
1 Samuel chapter 3 verses 1–19

There's a way back to
  God   248

John chapter 14 verses 5–14
Matthew chapter 7 verses 13–14
John chapter 1 verses 19–28

When I survey the
  wondrous
  cross   277

Psalm 22
Matthew chapter 27 verses 27–50
Luke chapter 23

Who is on the Lord's
  side?   287

Matthew chapter 12 verses 24–37
1 Samuel chapter 17 verses 1–51
Psalm 98
2 Timothy chapter 2 verses 1–10

Will your anchor
  hold   290

Psalm 62
Matthew chapter 8 verses 23–27
Mark chapter 6 verses 45–52

Lord we ask now to
  receive your
  blessing   301

Numbers chapter 6 verses 24–26
1 Corinthians chapter 13 verses
  1–8
John chapter 17 verses 11–13

Prayers for Commitment

Heavenly Father, I know that it's not enough just to say that I'm a Christian: you want my whole life to show that Jesus is my Lord, so that when others look at me, they will see that my life is different. You say in the Bible, 'Be holy, as I am holy', and that seems impossible. When so many people around me don't care about being holy and pure, it's difficult to be different. But I do want my life to please you, and I do want to be holy and pure in the way I live.

Please help me by your Holy Spirit to say 'No' to temptation, to say 'No' to following others when what they do is wrong, and help me to accept your standards and receive your power to keep to them.

In Jesus' Name, Amen.

Lord Jesus, It's easy to say I want to be a Christian because I want to go to heaven when I die, but it's not so easy to live as a Christian here among my friends and people who don't care about you. It would be a lot easier to be a Christian in secret and not to let anyone know, so that I wouldn't be laughed at or criticised for it. But I know that's not right: you say that if we are not prepared to acknowledge that we belong to you before people, you won't acknowledge that we belong to you before your Father. Please give me the courage to tell others about your love and to show by the way I live that you are my Lord.

I ask this for your glory, Amen.

Heavenly Father, I say that I want to go on as a Christian, but I know that there are many things in my life that don't help me to do that. Some of my friends who try to persuade me to do wrong; some of the books and magazines I read, and programmes I watch on television. They teach me things which I know are wrong and not pleasing to you, but I find it hard to leave them alone.

Please Lord, give me an eagerness to spend time doing things that will help me to become the person you want me to be. Help me to fill my mind with things that are good and pure; to put down books and magazines that fill me with wrong thoughts; to turn off the television if a programme is on that I know is unhelpful to watch. Please give me friends who also want to follow you, so that together we can enjoy the life that you give to us.

In Jesus' Name, Amen.

Lord Jesus, I have many dreams of what I'd like to do in the future; sometimes I dream of being rich and famous, sometimes of doing all the things I really enjoy doing, and sometimes of travelling to exciting places.

But sometimes I wonder what *you* would like me to do. I don't want to think about it too hard, because I know you wouldn't like some of my plans, especially the ones that would just make *me* happy.

If I'm going to follow you though, I've got to give you my future and let you lead me into whatever you want. Please start to make me willing for that.

In your Name, Amen.

Lord Jesus, You know what it's like to be unpopular. People mocked you, spat at you, told lies about you, and in the end killed you.

Thank you that you understand what it feels like to be rejected because of what you believe and the way you live your life. Sometimes when people laugh at me for being a Christian, I think that I'll give it all up and join in with them, but what I really want to do is to follow you.

Next time it happens, please help me to remember that you went through it too, and help me even to be glad that I can know a bit of how you felt, and let that bring me closer to you. Help me not to hate those who laugh at me: teach me to understand them and love them as you loved those who put you to death.

In your Name, Amen.

Lord Jesus, You told your disciples that if they really wanted to follow you they must love God with all their heart, with all their soul and with all their mind, and they must love their neighbour as they love themselves. Being your disciple today still involves that, and I want to learn to love, honour and obey you with every part of my life, and learn to love even the people I don't like.

Come into every part of my life, Lord Jesus, and make it your own.

In your Name, Amen.

Dear Lord Jesus, Sometimes it's hard to follow you and be a Christian. Some people laugh at me for believing in you, some say that God doesn't exist; some try to make me to do things that I know are wrong. But I do want to keep following you whatever other people say. Please give me the courage to keep going even when it is difficult. Thank you for promising that you will never leave me alone and help me to remember this whenever I am finding it hard to follow you, and to let you help me.

In your Name, Amen.

Dear Heavenly Father, Some of us decided to follow Jesus a long time ago and want to thank you for his faithfulness. Some of us were keen a while ago, but then the road seemed to be getting a bit difficult and we started to give up. And some of us have never made that most important decision to follow you. We pray that we will all have the courage to say 'yes' to Jesus – however hard it may seem and whatever *else* we may have to say 'no' to. We pray that we will keep our eyes firmly fixed on Him and grow to love Him more and more, so we will never even think of looking back. Jesus gave everything up for me. Help me give everything up for Him.

In His Name we ask this, Amen.

These doubts and uncertainties
are bothering me, Jesus,
One minute I can't help but believe in you,
the next minute I *need* help to believe in you.
You made faith, right?
Together with everything that is good?
Well, I need a bit,
now;
and I need to be made willing to use it.

Please help me, Jesus

Lord Jesus, I know that I have done many things that have been wrong, and that I need to be forgiven by you. Thank you that you died on the cross for me so that all my sins could be forgiven and so that I could be made clean from them all.

I'm sorry for all the wrong that I have done, and ask you now to forgive me. Please come by your Holy Spirit to live within me and make me your own. Thank you that you promise that whoever calls on your Name will be saved, and whoever confesses their sin to you will be forgiven and made clean. Thank you for your life within me which will keep me from doing what is wrong and will change me into the person you want me to be.

Thank you for your love and the fact that now there is nothing that can ever separate me from you.

Thank you for hearing my prayer.

Amen.

19 Confession

Cleanse me from my
   sin   27

2 Kings chapter 5 verses 1–14
Psalm 51
Mark chapter 1 verses 40–45

Search me, O
   God   212

Psalm 139
Psalm 51
1 John chapter 1 verse 5, chapter
   2 verse 2

Spirit of the living
   God   222

Acts chapter 2
Acts chapter 19 verses 1–6
John chapter 14 verses 15–26
Psalm 51

Prayers of Confession

Dear God, Sometimes when I've done things I know I shouldn't have done, I think you must be very angry with me and that you won't love me any more. But that's not true. The Bible tells us that you love us all the time, although you hate the bad things that we sometimes do. Thank you that your love for us is so great that you even sent your son Jesus to die so that we can be forgiven for all the wrong we have done. Thank you that you are a good and loving God.

In Jesus' Name, Amen.

Lord God, There seems to be so much hatred in the world today, and so much trouble. It's easy to blame you, Lord, for everything that happens, but the trouble starts in our own hearts with selfishness, pride and anger. Please forgive us for our wrong attitudes and help us to guard our hearts from these things that will spoil our lives.

In Jesus' Name, Amen.

Dear Father, Sometimes we can be very mean to other people: we laugh at them because they are different to us, or we won't let them be our friends because we don't like

the things they do. In your eyes each person is as special as
everyone else: you don't care what colour their skin is, or
what language they speak – they are all special to you. Please
forgive us for the times we have been unkind to others and
made them sad because they are different, and help us to
respect and love each person.

                                In Jesus' Name, Amen.

I'm in one of those couldn't-care-less moods, God.
I'm sorry.
That's just how I feel:
as if nothing matters.
I expect you might feel insulted
when I feel like this
but it happens from time to time.
Why?
Is it the same for everyone?
All sorts of words and phrases describe the way I feel:
indifference, apathy, disinterest,
and, come to think of it,
it is as if I actually feel nothing.
I'm sort of numb inside.

Wake me, Lord,
shake me up,
startle me.
You have so much at your elbow, God,
so many amazing things,
you ought to find it easy to disturb me,
to break this negative, destructive mood.

Being honest though
I'm not sure I want disturbing.
Help me.

I feel angry, God.
I know it's all right to feel worked up
about injustice, and war,
and terrorism and so on,
and I do care about all those things;

but, right now, I'm seething, boiling,
hopping made – I'm furious!
And you know why?
Somewhere inside me someone lit a fuse
and, unless you help me,
I'm going to go off with a very loud bang.
Calm me down, Lord;
help me sort out my feelings;
help me to be more like Jesus:
he stayed calm when all sorts of terrible things
were done to him,
when awful things were said about him;
help me to believe in you.
I need you.

I'm wicked, really, Lord.
It isn't even that I hate people,
or even dislike them,
I just love a good argument.
I enjoy the heat it generates.
I can warm myself at the fire;
the flames of conflict lick at my mind and I feel good.

I'm not even serious,
I'm smiling inside, especially when the other person
gets more and more angry.
My conscience does both me sometimes,
but I tend not to listen until it's too late,
and there are tears or, worse,
a broken relationship.

I'm sure you don't like me being like this, God,
and, sometimes, I wish I wasn't like it.
Could you strengthen the wish,
fulfil the desire?
I need you.

Father, So often we forget that it is you who provides all that
we need in our lives, and we forget to thank you for all that
you have given us. We thank you today for your love to us

and for the people who love us and look after us, thank you for keeping us well, and for our food and our toys. Thank you that you know what is best for each one of us.

In Jesus' Name, Amen.

Heavenly Father, It must have been hard for you to send your son and then watch Him being rejected by so many people. He's still being rejected by people who won't admit that He's right and they are wrong. I am sorry I've hurt you too by ignoring Jesus, by not standing up for what is right, by going the wrong way and even by lying sometimes. Forgive me and let me come back to you through His forgiveness, back to living a real life which is on track.

In Jesus' Name, Amen.

Oh Lord Jesus
I feel sad, miserable, downright unhappy.
You must have felt the same
when your friends betrayed you;
when people you had helped took you for granted,
and couldn't even be bothered to say 'Thank you';
so you must be able to understand how I feel.
Now there's a thought:
my sadness might help me
to understand my friends when they feel miserable.
Thanks, Jesus,
I feel a bit better already.

I don't have to tell you, Lord,
I'm lazy:
active as a fossil, I am!

I have trouble with my feet –
they prefer slippers to walking shoes!

Forgive me, Jesus.
You sweated blood for me.
You ask me to follow you but I prefer my comfort;
you place opportunities before me but I bury my head in
    my pillow;

you encourage me from within, putting thoughts in my
    mind,
but I nodd off.
Teach me, Lord, the folly of idleness,
that it hardens the arteries of a loving heart.

I'm praying, Lord, because, deep down,
I don't want to go on being lazy.
Change me.

I'm jealous,
emerald green with resentment.
Why that person and not me?
You know what I'm talking about, Jesus,
you know exactly.

Forgive me,
I can't help it.

A great many things around me actually encourage envy.
Phoney standards are drawn for me,
my attention is drawn to them over and over again;
it tends to be those who are after my money
and, even though I know what they're up to,
their lies are so very clever
and sound like truths.

Jealousy is so silly, Lord,
but knowing that doesn't stop me feeling it.
Be my distraction, Jesus,
win the battle for my eyes and ears and mind
Jesus, please help me,
jealousy can be so destructive.

You know what I've done,
Lord God,
and, no doubt, you're reminding me
that I need your help in putting the wrong thing right
I'm sorry.
Please forgive me.
Help me not to do the same thing again.

I expect you want me to apologise for what I've done.
That'll be hard.

So, Lord, as well as your forgiveness,
I need your help
and encouragement,
until I've done what's right.

O God, I feel rotten.
You know what I did,
and you know how lousy it's making me feel;
I didn't think I had much of a conscience,
till now. You'd think feelings as bad as this would stop
    me
doing wrong things
but the feeling wears off . . .
perhaps God, if I could understand *why*
certain things are wrong, and not just 'because you say
    so',
maybe then I'd want to be different,
I don't know. But I want to stop feeling rotten.
I'm sorry.

It was the most awful argument, Lord.
We hurt one another
with words – using words as weapons.
Forgive me, Lord.
I just hit out.
But now
we've made it up.
Thank you.
Not so long ago
I would have carried on the conflict,
the fight would've lasted longer,
till I thought I'd won, or
till I had the last word.
Thank you for helping me to control my tongue.
It seems I'll always need you.

Lord, I know that I do many wrong things but you are always so ready to forgive me. You accept me as I am and I just want to ask you to make me yours. I want you to come and live in me always, although I know that I don't deserve it. Please guide me daily so that I will do what you want me to do.

In your Name, Amen.

Father, Sometimes I am so bad and do naughty things. Even so you love and care for me and I want to belong to you. I know that so often I don't deserve your love, but please look after me each day. I want to ask you to come and to be in charge of my life, helping me to be good.

In Jesus' Name, Amen.

20 Friends and Family

Bind us together
Lord 17

1 Corinthians chapter 12 verses 12–27
Ephesians chapter 4 verses 2–6
John chapter 17 verses 6–12, 20–23
1 John chapter 2 verses 7–11, chapter 4 verses 7–12

Brothers and
sisters 21

Galatians chapter 3 verse 26, chapter 4 verse 7
Ephesians chapter 4 verses 1–16
Psalm 133

Father I place into your
hands 42

Psalm 25
Psalm 139
Deuteronomy chapter 33 verses 26–29
Matthew chapter 6 verses 25–34

For the beauty of the
earth 48

Genesis chapter 1 verses 1–31
2 Peter chapter 1 verses 3–9
Psalm 8

Have you seen the
pussycat? 72

Psalm 104
Psalm 65
Luke chapter 8 verses 41–56

He's got the whole
wide world in His
hands 78

Psalm 24
Genesis chapter 8 verse 21, chapter 9 verse 17
Deuteronomy chapter 33 verse 26–29

In our work and in our
play 108

Luke chapter 2 verses 41–52
Galatians chapter 5 verses 16–26
Mark chapter 10 verses 13–16

It's me, it's me, it's me
O Lord 117

Matthew chapter 11 verses 25–30
Luke chapter 8 verses 41–56
Luke chapter 18 verses 1–8

Jesus is a friend of
   mine 136

John chapter 15 verses 12–17
John chapter 11 verses 1–44
Romans chapter 5 verses 1–11

Shalom my friend 217

John chapter 14 verses 23–31
Psalm 29
Isaiah chapter 26 verses 3–12

Lord we ask now to
   receive your
   blessing 301

Numbers chapter 6 verses 24–26
1 Corinthians chapter 13 verses
  1–18
John chapter 17 verses 11–13

Prayers for Friends and Family

Lord, There are some days when I feel as though I want to run away from all my friends and family and everyone I know just to be alone, away from all these people who are a part of my life. I'd like to see what it's like without them, to be on my own in the world.

And yet there are other days when I really want to be with them all, and when I have to go away from home I miss them and get lonely. It's easy to take friends and family for granted and to get fed up with them when I'm with them all the time. Show me ways of getting to know them better so there will be new ways of enjoying their company.

Amen.

Heavenly Father, You want us to learn to care about our friends and to show them that we *are* their friends even when everything goes wrong for them. Please give us the kind of love for people that you have, so that even when our friends hurt us or get themselves into trouble, we will still stick by them.

We pray for any of our friends who are ill today or unhappy in any way. Please be close to them and let them know that you love them. Show us what we can do to help them.

In Jesus' Name, Amen.

Lord Jesus, I get angry with my friends sometimes, because I expect them all to be just like me and to enjoy doing the things I enjoy. You have made us all so different though, so that some of us are good at sport, some at music, some at studying. Please teach us to learn to enjoy the fact that we are different in many ways and help us learn from our friends instead of trying to make them like us.

Thank you Lord, Amen.

Lord, I've had such a good time with my friends today. We've done lots of great things and laughed a lot together. It wouldn't have been half so much fun on my own. Thank you Lord for each one of them.

Amen.

Lord, Today I just needed someone to talk to. Someone who wouldn't try to give me advice, or tell me what I should be doing. just someone who would listen to me and care about the way I was feeling. That's why it's so good to have friends. Thank you for the people who are such good friends to me.

Amen.

Lord, There are some people at school who don't seem to have many friends. They must get very lonely. If you were here I think you would be their friend so please help me to look out for them and to be a friend to them.

In your Name, Amen.

Dear God, You are the best friend anyone can ever have because you always want the best for us, and you are always there to look after us and help us. Thank you for wanting to be our friend even when no-one else wants to be. Thank you for caring for each one of us.

There are so many people today who don't have anyone to care for them, and we pray that you will help them to know that you see them and you care for them.

In Jesus' Name, Amen.

Dear Lord, So often it's easy to quarrel with people even though they are our friends or our family. Thank you that you can help us to make friends again with people and not let our arguments separate us from each other. We are sorry for the times we make others unhappy because of what we say and do, and ask you to forgive us. Please give us your love to love others with.

In Jesus' Name, Amen.

Dear Heavenly Father, I know that sometimes I love my family and friends a lot, and want to do things to help them; but other times I don't love them very much at all. In the Bible it says, 'A friend loves at all times'. Please help me to learn how to love people all the time –even if they have hurt me or if they don't love me. Thank you that your love for us is always the same and that you never love us less because of anything that we do. It's so good to know that there is someone who loves us all the time.

Thank you Lord, Amen.

Jesus, it never dawned on me before,
not like this anyway –
that friends are precious.
Thank you for letting me see
how much my friends mean to me.
Help me to be a friend
who can be relied upon.
Amen.

Lord, I'm finding myself hard to understand;
see, there are nearly four billion people
crammed onto this planet, and yet,
somehow or other, I feel lonely!
You must have felt lonely
when you said your Father had left you,
you know, when you were dying.
Jesus, never let me be *that* lonely, please;
I couldn't bear it, not like you did.
Daft as it might seem, with all these people about,
I do feel lonely.
I'm just telling you honestly how I feel.
So, please help me, Jesus,
I need you as a friend.

I feel as if nobody loves me.
Honest to God, that's how I feel, Jesus.
I'm told you love me always, for ever,
that my parents love me,
but that's not how I feel.
I'm hurting inside.
I feel alone, lost, on my own:
that's how I feel.

I suppose I know you love me,
and so do other people,
but, right now,
my feeling doesn't match my knowing;
oh, I don't know what I feel!
To say
'Everybody is against me'
is an exaggeration, but
it is how I feel.
I think.
Please help me.

Some people might call me 'smug', Jesus,
but you know I'm not;
I'm just pleased.
I found pleasure in something,
it was beautiful,
I'd never seen anything like it;
I was given enjoyment by someone,
just being with them was good,
getting to know them,
listening to them,
watching them,
seeing who they were.
They seemed to enjoy being with me;
we were pleased to be together.
I still feel pleased,
thinking about them.
Thank you.

If it's true that you feel love, God,
love towards everything you have made,
then, Lord, perhaps you know

how I'm feeling,
only more so
I feel high, tingly, excited.
I think I'm in love.

Have you brought us together, God?
Are we right for one another?
Can it possibly last a lifetime?
Is it too good to be true?
Am I asking the right questions?

Help me to understand what is happening;
help me not to depend too much on feelings
(though I thank you for them, I feel good!);
help me to distinguish truth from fantasy,
you know I tend to dream a bit;
help me not to shut you out if this new relationship;
we're going to need you.
You *are* love.

Dear Lord, Sometimes I get so unhappy at home, but it doesn't seem right to tell anyone that. Thank you that you know all about it. You know the things that make me cry and hurt inside. Thank you that you are my Heavenly Father and that you love me with a love which is far greater than any human love could ever be. Help me to hang on to your love when things are bad, and I feel that no one cares.

Thank you Lord, Amen.

Heavenly Father, I love being with my family. We have such great times together, and we really feel as though we belong together. Thank you for each one of them.

Amen.

Dear Lord, My mum's expecting a new baby and it makes me feel jealous sometimes. I keep thinking that everyone will only be interested in the baby now, and that they won't care about me. I know it's not true, it's just a feeling I have. I want to love our new baby as well and help to look after it. Please make me a good brother/sister.

Amen.

Lord, Thank you for our parents. Thank you for the way they look after us by providing all that we need, spending time doing things for us, and giving up many things they would like to have for our sakes. Please teach us to be obedient to them and to respect them for all that they do. Help us to find ways of saying thank you to them for all they mean to us.

In your Name, Amen.

Dear Lord, Soon I'll be leaving my family to go away to college. I've never been away from home for that long before, and I think I'm going to get homesick and miss my family. Please look after them all while I'm away and help me always to feel part of the family even though I'm living away from home. Help me to remember those whom I leave behind, and write letters to them to show I care about them. Thank you that even though I won't have my family with me, you will be there to look after me.

Thank you Lord, Amen.

21   God in Creation

All things bright and beautiful 6	Genesis chapters 1–2 verse 3 Psalm 19 Psalm 65 Psalm 104 Psalm 148
All around me Lord 7	Psalm 19 verses 1–14 Romans chapter 1 verses 18–23 Romans chapter 8 verses 18–23
For the beauty of the earth 48	Genesis chapter 1 verses 1–31 2 Peter chapter 1 verses 3–9 Psalm 8
God whose farm is all creation 61	Psalm 24 Matthew chapter 13 verses 1–23 Haggai chapter 1 verses 5–7
God who made the earth 63	Genesis chapter 1 verses 1–31 2 Peter chapter 1 verses 3–9 Matthew chapter 8 verses 23–27
He made the stars to shine 76	Colossians chapter 1 verses 12–22 Genesis chapter 1 verses 1–31 1 Peter chapter 1 verses 17–21
In the stars his handiwork I see 112	Psalm 19 Job chapter 38 verses 1–11, 22–29, chapter 42 verses 1–6 John chapter 10 verses 11–14, 27–30
It came upon the midnight clear 116	Luke chapter 2 verses 8–14 Luke chapter 2 verses 21–35
O Lord my God 179	Psalm 8 Romans chapter 5 verses 9–11 1 Thessalonians chapter 4 verses 16–17 John chapter 3 verses 16–18

Remember all the people 207	Acts chapter 1 verses 1–8 Romans chapter 10 verses 13–17 2 Peter chapter 3 verses 1–9
Stand up, clap hands 225	Psalm 150 Acts chapter 3 verses 1–11 Psalm 23
Who put the colours in the rainbow? 288	Genesis chapter 9 verses 8–16 Ecclesiastes chapter 12 verses 1–7 Job chapter 38 verses 1–12, 34–41 Romans chapter 1 verses 18–23 Psalm 104 verses 1–24

Prayers about God in Creation

Yesterday, Lord, I was feeling fed up. I looked out and it was raining. The sky was dark with heavy clouds. I looked from them down to a small drop of water hanging on a leaf edge, just about to fall. Where did this greatness and smallness come from? People have told me it just happened. I don't think so. I blink at the glare of the sun and then focus on a ladybird trundling along a blade of grass and something in me just has to shout, 'Thank you Heavenly Father, you have made it all, and more than that you gave me eyes to see. Never let me get too proud to stop seeing and stop thanking!'

You're a wonderful God. Amen.

Dear Lord, Thank you for giving to us all the wonders of creation. Thank you for the flowers and the animals we see day by day. Help us Lord to learn to appreciate all that you have given us and thank you that you show yourself to us through the beauty of everything around us.

Amen.

Heavenly Father, We want to praise you because you are God. We praise you because you made this world and everything that is in it. You made the sun and moon, the earth and sea, all the animals and the trees and flowers and you made us. We praise you because you have made everything so beautiful and given us so much to enjoy. Help us to remember how special everything is because you made it and teach us to take care of your world and all that is in it.

In Jesus' Name, Amen.

Dear Father, You have made such a beautiful world with so many wonderful things for us to see and enjoy. Even in the middle of a town we can find things that you have made – the birds who come to our gardens, the trees and flowers in the park, the grass that sometimes grows up through the cracks in the pavement. Thank you that wherever we live we can see so much that reminds us what a great creator you are.

In Jesus' Name, Amen.

Heavenly Father, We praise you because you have created a world that is beautiful and awe-inspiring. When we think about the size of the universe, or when we hear the sound of crashing thunder or feel the power of waves breaking on the seashore we remember what a great God you are. And then we see the little things like the pattern on a butterfly's wing, the colours of the feathers on a duck, the different shapes of leaves on the trees, and we realise that as well as being a very powerful and mighty God, you also care about little details, and have a great sense of beauty. Please teach us to appreciate all that you have made and to enjoy this world.

In Jesus' Name, Amen.

Dear God, Thank you for such a wonderful world, and thank you for giving us the ability to enjoy all that you have made. It's good to be able to see the beauty of your creation; the colours and designs; to hear the different sounds of birds' songs, water trickling along a stream, a baby crying. Thank you for the gift of taste: food would be so dull without all the flavours you have made. Thank you for inventing the sense of smell which makes things so special: the smell of woodsmoke on bonfire night, or of pine needles at Christmas time.

Thank you too for the ability to touch and feel your creation with the many textures, shapes and sizes. Thank you for how good it feels to be hugged by a friend.

We praise you for all these things and for the way that your creation teaches us more about yourself.

In Jesus' Name, Amen.

Thank you God for all the beautiful and wonderful things you have made. You made the sun, trees, mountains, other planets – so many things bigger and more complicated than our minds can ever understand. We can feel so small when we think of the world you have made. But thank you, that people are the most special part of your creation because you created them in your image and they can talk to you and get to know you. Thank you that we know how special *we* are because you made us.

In Jesus' Name, Amen.

Dear Father in Heaven, Please forgive us that sometimes we get so worried about things that shouldn't be important to us. We worry about what we look like, about having the latest fashions, and having as many clothes as our friends have. When you made us, you made us look the way that pleases you: please help us to accept that and to know that because we are created by you, we are beautiful. Help us not to want to be different to the way you made us and help us not to think that we need lots of clothes and make-up to make us attractive. Thank you that in some ways we are like the flowers you made: all different, but all beautiful in their own way.

In Jesus' Name Amen.

Father, We are so glad to know that this world and all that happens in it, is under your control. Thank you that when you had created this earth and the people on it, you didn't go away and leave us to try to run the world on our own, but you have plans and purposes for this world that you are working out. Thank you that nothing can stop your plans for this world and one day, when the Lord Jesus comes back everyone will turn to Him and He will reign as King over the whole world and there will be peace on earth.

Thank you.

In Jesus' Name, Amen.

Heavenly Father, We thank you that you made every person in the world and that each one is very special to you. We thank you that you have made each person differently so that no-one is quite like anyone else. Thank you for the people from different countries who may be different from us in many ways: in the way they dress, their language, the food they eat, the customs they have, and in the colour of their skin. Thank you that we can all learn so much from one another, and please teach us to love one another just as you love us all.

In Jesus' Name, Amen.

You made a beautiful world, Lord, and we can all enjoy it if we only open our eyes. Forgive us when we start to take things for granted and don't thank you that the stars come out every night and the sea seems to know where to stop as it crashes onto the beach.

Thank you you're not just a God of creation but a God of love. Thank you that you showed how much you loved us by sending Jesus, your only son, to die for us. Thank you that you stepped into your creation and you know all about pain and suffering and death as well as beauty and hope and life.

Help us never to forget to look up and say 'thank you'.

In Jesus' Name, Amen.

Your world, your creation, God,
it's mind-blowing!
Variety, beauty, colour, contrasts:
unique snowflakes which melt on my fingers,
mountains more than five miles high,
oceans and icicles,
forests and fir-cones,
deserts and . . . er, egg-timers.
Your universe, God,
I'm all agog!
From the invisible to the unimaginable,
and, amongst all this,
me,
and my family, and my friends,

and people like me all over the world.
For the fact that everywhere there is something good,
thank you, God.

Dear God, Sometimes I wonder why I am here on earth, and who made me. When I look at everything in the world around me I realise that it must have been made by someone who is very clever, and also by someone who loves beautiful things, because the things I see are too wonderful just to have been formed by chance. Thank you that you loved what you had created so much that when you saw that it was being spoilt by sin you cared enough to send Jesus to die so that you could reclaim from Satan everything that belongs to you. Thank you that because Jesus died for me, I can know you as the one who made me, and as my Father in Heaven.
Thank you in Jesus' Name, Amen.

Thank you, Heavenly Father, that you care about the smallest details: we can see that in the world around us – the shimmering stripes on a fish's side, the tiny bee gathering particles of pollen. So many wonders all around. Thank you that you also care about the details in our lives. The way we speak to people – the things we enjoy. The hurts that go deep. We pray for anyone who doesn't know you. We pray they will look around and realise you care as much for them as the rest of your beautiful creation.
Amen.

22 Guidance

Ask! Ask! Ask! and it shall be given you 11

Luke chapter 11 verses 5–13
Luke chapter 12 verses 22–34
Matthew chapter 7 verses 7–14

Be bold 14

Exodus chapters 3 and 4
Joshua chapter 1 verses 6–9
Deuteronomy chapter 31 verses 1–8
1 John chapter 4 verses 11–18
1 Samuel chapter 17 verses 1–58

Do you want a Pilot? 40

Luke chapter 8 verses 22–25
Ecclesiastes chapter 11 verse 9, chapter 12 verse 7
John chapter 10 verses 1–14, 27–30

Father I place into your hands 42

Psalm 25
Psalm 139
Deuteronomy chapter 13 verses 26–29
Matthew chapter 6 verses 25–34

Father, lead me day by day 43

Luke chapter 4 verses 1–14
Mark chapter 1 verses 9–13
Exodus chapter 14 verses 1–31

God is our guide 56

Psalm 25 verses 4–15
Jude chapters 20–25
Proverbs chapter 3 verses 1–13
Psalm 27
Exodus chapter 13 verses 17–22

God is working His purpose out 57

Isaiah chapter 11 verses 1–10
Isaiah chapter 55 verses 6–11
1 Thessalonians chapter 4 verse 13, chapter 5 verse 11
Jonah (extracts)

I am trusting you Lord   John chapter 14 verses 1–6, 15–21
    Jesus   86   Psalm 25
                              Proverbs chapter 3 verses 1–7
                              Luke chapter 8 verses 41–56

I know who holds the   Matthew chapter 6 verses 23–34
    future   92   Psalm 48
                              Isaiah chapter 58 verses 8–14

I have decided to   Luke chapter 9 verses 57–62
    follow Jesus   98   1 John chapter 2 verses 15–17
                              Luke chapter 14 verses 25–33
                              Luke chapter 5 verses 27–32

One more step along   Psalm 48
    the world I go   188   John chapter 10 verses 11–18,
                                  27–30
                              Romans chapter 12 verses 1–2
                              Philippians chapter 4 verses 4–9

Put your hand in the   Matthew chapter 8 verses 23–27
    hand   206   Luke chapter 5 verses 1–11
                              John chapter 2 verses 13–17

The Lord's my   Psalm 23
    shepherd   243   John chapter 10 verses 1–21
                              Luke chapter 15 verses 1–7

When the road is rough   Isaiah chapter 42 verses 1–2
    and steep   279   Matthew chapter 14 verses 22–33
                              Matthew chapter 28 verses 16–20
                              Daniel chapter 3 verses 1–28

Will your anchor   Psalm 62
    hold?   290   Matthew chapter 8 verses 23–27
                              Mark chapter 6 verses 45–52

Your hand O God has   Ephesians chapter 4 verses 1–6
    guided   298   Matthew chapter 22 verses 1–14
                              Exodus chapter 13 verses 18–22,
                                  chapter 14 verses 1–31
                              Psalm 145

Prayers for Guidance

Lord Jesus, Your greatest desire was to please your Father
in heaven. So often *my* greatest desire is to better myself and
forget what you have to say about the things I want! Help
me Lord to consider your ways and your thoughts before I
jump into making decisions because I can so easily mess
things up. Thank you for hearing my prayer.

Amen.

So many voices, Jesus,
all claiming to have the solutions to life's problems.
I get confused.

There are sensible voices,
religious voices,
persuasive voices,
political voices,
everywhere, Lord, on radio and television,
in newspapers and magazines,
different voices.
Help me, Lord, to tell the difference
between what makes sense and what is right,
between what is 'good' and what is God.

I just thought of something funny,
I hope you don't mind –
GOOD is GOD with nothing added!
Or GOD is GOOD with nothing taken away.
It's not funny, is it? But it's right,
it's true.
Help me to want all of you, Lord,
nothing taken away;
help me to see you like that;
that'd be the beginning of the end of my confusion.
Help me to hear your voice.

Lord Jesus, Thank you that you come into our lives to guide
us and show us the way that we should go. Thank you that

the way that you have planned for us is the best way. Please help us to follow you and not just do the things that we want to do.

In your Name, Amen.

Sometimes Lord, things can be very confusing. One of my friends says, 'This is the right thing to do,' and another says, 'No, this is the right one.' Everyone has their own ideas and I can't always see which one is right. Thank you that you said, 'I am *the* way,' not '*a* way'. Thank you that you leave no doubt. If we don't allow you to be the way for us to God, then we aren't going anywhere, we don't know anything and we're not living a life that has any point. But thank you that when we admit you are the way, we are secure and happy now and forever.

In your Name, Amen.

I'm not exactly afraid of the future, God,
but I am worried.
I worry about all kinds of things.
Sometimes I worry about being worried!
Perhaps,
if I really believed you are in charge of things,
even though it doesn't look like it sometimes,
perhaps then I wouldn't worry so much.
Maybe I need to believe in you more:
more truly, more deeply, more often.
I do trust you, Lord,
but please help me
to trust you more.

I have a decision to make, Jesus,
and I don't know what to do.
If it was black and white it wouldn't be a problem,
well, not *understanding* what to do; though
actually *doing* it might be difficult.
Just now I'm trying to sort out the first bit:
right from wrong, or even
right from right.

I'm glad I have the chance to choose,
it is a luxury,
but I do need help with the choosing.
It would help me, Lord.
If you would make it clear to me –
what *you* want.
Will you?
Please.

You hesitated once, Jesus,
as death approached,
and you wondered over possibilities.
I'm hanging back,
hesitant, afraid, unsure.
I need your help, Lord,
as I make up my mind,
because I want to do right.
Right is what you want me to do,
so please
help me

So many pressures on me, God,
pushing this way and that,
threatening to tear me apart;
that's how I feel.

Teachers, parents, friends,
magazines, television, advertising,
ambition, impatience, frustration,
they get me all tied up inside,
good and evil staging a tug-of-war in my mind.

Help me to see tension positively:
stress exercises and strengthens muscles.
Help me to grow stronger through pressure,
save me from giving in when I should be going on.

I feel all mixed up, Lord,
I need sorting out,
in my mind.
I need you to sort me out,
and then to go on helping me.

Heavenly Father, It's so funny to watch a field of sheep. They can all be wandering around the field and then suddenly they all start following one sheep and running after each other! It shows that they need a shepherd to watch over them and guide them or they would all get lost. Lord, I can so easily follow the way of other people instead of looking to you as the Good Shepherd who wants to guide and protect His flock. I don't want to be like a wandering sheep which doesn't know where it's going: please teach me to hear your voice and follow after you.

In Jesus' Name, Amen.

Dear Lord, Please give me a real sense of direction in my life. I know that you have many good things planned for me, but I need to learn to obey you and be prepared to do the things you want. I know that as I trust you and obey you, you will lead me and guide me so that I will know what you want me to do with my life.

Thank you Lord, Amen.

23 Health and Healing

Be still and know that I
  am God   22

Psalm 46
John chapter 14 verses 23–27
Luke chapter 8 verses 22–25
Luke chapter 10 verses 38–42
Ecclesiastes chapter 3 verses 1–11

Cleanse me from my
  sin, Lord   27

2 Kings chapter 5 verses 1–14
Psalm 51
Mark chapter 1 verses 40–45
Psalm 38

Come to Jesus, He's
  amazing   33

Mark chapter 10 verses 13–16
Luke chapter 18 verses 15–18

Dear Lord and father of
  mankind   37

Romans chapter 12 verses 1–8
Matthew chapter 4 verses 18–22
Genesis chapter 27 verses 1–46

In the name of
  Jesus   111

Luke chapter 4 verses 1–13
1 John chapter 5 verses 1–5
Matthew chapter 8 verses 28–34

Live, live, live   153

Isaiah chapter 53
John chapter 9 verses 1–25
Acts chapter 17 verses 22–28

Make me a channel of
  your peace   161

Psalm 37 verses 1–11
Matthew chapter 5 verses 1–16
2 Corinthians chapter 1 verses 2–7
Matthew chapter 6 verses 9–15
Mark chapter 8 verses 34–38

May the mind of Christ
  my Saviour   165

Philippians chapter 2 verses 1–11
Psalm 1
Psalm 119 verses 1–16
John chapter 14 verses 23–28

Oh, oh, oh, how good
  is the Lord   180

Acts chapter 3 verses 1–16
Ephesians chapter 1 verses 3–14
Psalm 103

Peace I give to you 196	John chapter 14 verses 23–31 John chapter 7 verses 37–39 1 Corinthians chapter 13 verses 1–8
Peter and John went to pray 198	Acts chapter 3 verses 1–11
There's new life in Jesus 249	1 John chapter 5 verses 1, 9–13 Psalm 32 Matthew chapter 9 verses 18–26 John chapter 11 verses 1–44
Turn your eyes upon Jesus 260	Colossians chapter 3 verses 1–17 Luke chapter 9 verses 27–36 Revelation chapter 1 verses 9–18

Prayers for Health and Healing

Dear God, Sometimes we want to see you perform miracles just like Jesus did when He lived on earth, and we forget that every day, all around us, you are causing miracles to take place. When we cut a finger, it's a miracle that it is able to heal itself by joining the cut together. When we break a bone, it's a miracle that the crack is repaired by the bone cells. When we get a virus or sickness, it's a miracle that our bodies produce cells and chemicals to kill the virus and protect us from disease.

Lord, our whole bodies, the way they work, and the way they heal themselves, are miracles in themselves and we thank you that if only we open our eyes to it, we can see you do miracles every day.

In Jesus' Name, Amen.

Lord God, A question that so many people ask is, 'How can God allow so much sickness and suffering?' It's hard to answer Lord, because you are a God of love and that must mean that you only want what's best for us. Sometimes people make themselves ill because of the kind of life they live, and sometimes people bring accidents on themselves because they don't take enough care, but there are some who seem to get ill for no reason. Even when we don't understand why people are sick, we can thank you that you have something to teach them through it and know that you will be with them and care for them.

Thank you Lord, Amen.

Heavenly Father, Usually we forget to thank you for our health until we become sick or hurt ourselves, and then we suddenly realise how important it is to us to be well.

Thank you today for our bodies and for our good health; jhelp us to look after our bodies, remembering that you want us to use them for your glory.

In Jesus' Name, Amen.

Lord, We want to pray today for those people who we know are sick or in hospital. We ask that today each one of them would be aware of your love for them, and that they would turn to you for strength to face their sickness. Help them not to be unhappy because they are unwell, but to learn something special about You during this time. We pray for (insert names).

In Jesus' Name, Amen.

Lord, It's strange, but when I do things that I know are wrong, it leaves me feeling rotten inside and sometimes it makes me feel quite sick and unwell when I think about what I've done.

Thank you that because you died for us on the cross, you are able to forgive our sins when we confess them to you and then you also take away the fear and guilt and make us clean and new inside again. Thank you that your forgiveness sets us free from our sin and makes us whole again.

In Jesus' Name, Amen.

I didn't know pain could be as bad as this.
Oh,
it hurts, Lord.
A teacher said 'Pain is good,
it's the body's warning signal.'
I don't feel good!

Why is my body shouting at me like this?
What have I done?
Or not done?
Do I need to put a higher value on health?
Take more care of my body?

I believe you made the human body, Lord,
made it good.
Can you make good out of my body,
even though I've neglected it?

Show me how to repect what you have made,
teach me to learn from this pain, Lord.
Forgive me.

I didn't enjoy being under the weather, God,
but I feel better now.
Thank you.
Teach me how to help others
who suffer, and
thank you for those who were good to me,
who helped me to feel better.

Help me never to forget
that there are people around me
who will never feel better;
help me to help them feel good.
Thinking of others doesn't come easy, Lord,
so I'll need you.

I used to be a tense sort of person, God,
but you showed me how to trust you.
Now,
I'm learning to let you take the strain,
I am learning to unwind.
I feel relaxed.
It's a good feeling.
Thank you, Lord.

Thank you Lord for being so concerned about children – I pray today that you will give comfort to children who are in hospital and those who are mentally and physically handicapped. Give them a special joy although they cannot take part in activities in the same way as we do. Even though we will never understand why people suffer in this way we pray that you will help them to know your peace and love in an extra special way – we ask this in your Name.

Amen.

Father, We thank you that you have made everything and that you know how everything works. We pray especially for those people who are blind and cannot see what you have made. We pray for those who are deaf and cannot hear the birds singing and the waves crashing. We pray for all those people who are less fortunate than ourselves. Thank you Lord for our health and strength and for our food and clothing.

In Jesus' Name, Amen.

It's all gone wrong, Lord,
the bottom has fallen out of my world.
I'm heartbroken.

Just yesterday my heart was full of love,
of faith, of hope,
but then my heart was broken
and its contents spilled out.
I feel utterly empty.

How could you deliberately empty yourself, Jesus?
They say that
when your heart was broken
blood and water poured out.
I've thought about that:
blood gives life and water gives health;
well, my life needs healing.
Can you heal broken hearts, Jesus?
I need you.

24 Missions

All over the world   5

Isaiah chapter 11 verses 1–9
Joel chapter 2 verses 23–32

Colours of day   28

Matthew chapter 5 verses 13–16
John chapter 1 verses 1–18
John chapter 8 verses 12

Come let us sing of a
   wonderful love   29

John chapter 3 verses 1–21
1 John chapter 3 verses 16–24
John chapter 6 verses 1–11

Come on, let's get up
   and go   31

Romans chapter 10 verses 13–17
John chapter 4 verses 1–42
Psalm 100
Isaiah chapter 35 verses 1–10

Come to Jesus, He's
   amazing   33

Mark chapter 10 verses 13–16
Luke chapter 18 verses 15–18

Father, I place into
   your hands   42

Psalm 25
Psalm 139
Deuteronomy chapter 33 verses
   26–29
Matthew chapter 6 verses 25–34

For I'm building a
   people of power   47

Ephesians chapter 2 verses 11–22
Psalm 149
John chapter 17 verses 1, 13–23
Matthew chapter 16 verses 13–20

God forgave my
   sin   54

Psalm 32
Matthew chapter 6 verses 9–15
Ephesians chapter 4 verses 17–32
Matthew chapter 10 verses 1–15
Luke chapter 21 verses 1–4

God is working His
   purpose out   57

Isaiah chapter 11 verses 1–10
Isaiah chapter 55 verses 6–11
1 Thessalonians chapter 4 verse
   13, chapter 5 verse 11
Jonah (extracts)

Go, tell it on the mountain 65

Romans chapter 10 verses 9–15
Philippians chapter 2 verses 1–11
Isaiah chapter 52 verses 7–10
Acts chapter 1 verses 1–8

How lovely on the mountains 84

Isaiah chapter 52 verses 7–10
Revelation chapter 19 verses 4–7
Isaiah chapter 54 verses 1–14
Matthew chapter 28 verses 16–20

I'm singing for my Lord 105

Acts chapter 16 verses 16–34
1 Corinthians chapter 9 verses 16–23
Psalm 47

I serve a risen Saviour 113

Matthew chapter 28 verses 1–9
John chapter 11 verses 1–27
Romans chapter 5 verses 1–10
Hebrews chapter 5 verses 5a–8

Isaiah heard the voice of the Lord 114

Isaiah chapter 6 verses 1–13

I will make you fishers of men 123

Luke chapter 5 verses 1–11
Matthew chapter 4 verses 18–22
John chapter 1 verses 35–51
John chapter 21 verses 1–8

Jesus bids us shine 128

Luke chapter 11 verses 33–36
John chapter 1 verses 1–12
John chapter 8 verses 12
Isaiah chapter 59 verses 1–2, 8–10, chapter 60 verses 1–3

Jesus died for all the children 132

John chapter 3 verses 14–17
Mark chapter 10 verses 13–16

Joy is the flag flying high 144

Acts chapter 3 verses 1–8
Philippians chapter 4 verses 4–9
Nehemiah chapter 8 verses 1–12

Let's talk about Jesus 150

John chapter 14 verses 1–6
John chapter 10 verses 1–9
Ephesians chapter 1 verses 15–23

Make me a channel of
your peace   161

Psalm 37 verses 1–11
Matthew chapter 5 verses 1–16
2 Corinthians chapter 1 verses 2–7
Matthew chapter 6 verses 9–15
Mark chapter 8 verses 34–38

Remember all the
people   207

Acts chapter 1 verses 1–8
Romans chapter 10 verses 13–17
2 Peter chapter 3 verses 1–9

Stand up, stand up for
Jesus   226

Ephesians chapter 6 verses 10–20
2 Timothy chapter 2 verses 1–10
1 Corinthians chapter 9 verses
   24–27
Romans chapter 8 verses 35–39

Tell out my soul   229

Mark chapter 5 verses 1–20
John chapter 4 verses 1–42
Psalm 30

The fields are
white   237

John chapter 4 verses 31–38
John chapter 4 verses 1–42
Luke chapter 10 verses 1–12
Revelation chapter 14 verses 13–20
Matthew chapter 13 verses 24–30

Though the world has
forsaken God   257

Matthew chapter 7 verses 13–20
John chapter 13 verses 31–35
Acts chapter 2 verses 14–21, 41–47
Joshua chapter 2 verses 1–21

This little light of
mine   258

Matthew chapter 5 verses 13–16
1 John chapter 1 verses 5–10
Isaiah chapter 60 verses 1–3, 19–22
John chapter 1 verses 1–13

We have heard a joyful
sound   266

Luke chapter 18 verses 1–10
Acts chapter 4 verses 5–12
Isaiah chapter 45 verses 18–25
1 Timothy chapter 2 verses 1–5

We've a story to tell to   Isaiah chapter 59 verse 1, chapter
  the nations   272   60 verse 3
                               Psalm 33
                               Isaiah chapter 2 verses 1–5

When I needed a   Matthew chapter 25 verses 31–46
  neighbour   275   Luke chapter 10 verses 30–37

Prayers about Mission

Lord, We pray today for those we know who are working to tell others about you, both in this country and abroad. We remember . . . (insert names and needs).

Thank you that you are with each one of them watching over them and providing for their needs. Please encourage them today in their work and remind them of your love.

In Jesus' Name, Amen.

Heavenly Father, There are so many people in the world who do not know you and your love. Sometimes it seems that there are too many people to pray for, but we want to begin to praying for our town/city . . . (insert name). We ask that you will bring many people in . . . (name) to put their trust in you. Please help them to see that they need you, and bring people into their lives who can tell them about your love.

In Jesus' Name, Amen.

Father, Help us to remember as we try to tell others about your love, that we are not here just to give the gospel, but to be the gospel. We pray that because of our lives many people will be attracted to you, and as we let others see what you have done in us to change us, they will want to see you do those things in them.

For Jesus' Sake, Amen.

Lord Jesus, You say that if we believe in you, rivers of everlasting life will flow out from us because of your life in us. Help us to keep that river pure and clean so that many people will be refreshed by our lives and will taste something of your life as they get to know us.

Thank you, Lord. Amen.

Heavenly Father, When I hear the story of you sending Jesus to die for me and set me free, it almost seems too wonderful to be true. Thank you that is why it is wonderful – because it is true. Whatever happens in life, however hard and dark some days may seem, I can know Jesus with me in every situation. And how amazing – you've promised that if I know you, you will take me to heaven when I die!

We pray for all the people who are telling others about Jesus. We pray they won't get discouraged and thank you that one day they will see in heaven all those they led to you.

In Jesus' Name, Amen.

You make me feel good, Lord,
and I'm satisfied.

I've noticed you and appreciated you
in love between people,
in loyalty amongst friends,
in kindness, in care, in concern, in compassion.

I tend to get caught up in the bad news,
the headlines in the papers,
and, when I do, I don't see you any more.

Bad news gets us all down, Lord,
it's depressing.
Help us to do something about it,
to create more good news,
to tip the scales the other way.
If you want to use me as you answer this prayer,
here I am, God,
use me.
And thank you for satisfying me.

Heavenly Father, We pray that you will help us to understand your plans and purposes for this world. Sometimes the world seems to be in such a mess but we know that you are at work, bringing people into your kingdom and showing them how to live as you want them to. Help us to tell more people about your love for them and the way they can come into your kingdom through Jesus so that your plans may be worked out and your kingdom come on earth.

In Jesus' Name, Amen.

Thank you, Lord God, for allowing me to hear the story of Jesus; how He came to die so that I could be forgiven and come to know you as my Father and my friend. Thank you that you loved me enough to allow Jesus to come to earth and die for me. I know that there are a lot of people who haven't heard about the way that you love them; please show me how you can use me to show others so that they will come to know you as well.

In Jesus' Name, Amen.

I have this guilt-feeling, Lord,
every time I see pictures from the third world.
I'm too well-off.
I thought I was hard done by
until I saw the poverty in parts of Africa
and South America
Forgive me, Lord.

My guilt may be unnecessary,
I don't know,
but I'm sure that me feeling guilty won't achieve much,
not if I just feel *guilty*.
I need to feel compassion, Lord,
I need to believe that I can do something to help,
I need to let go of my personal ambition,
I need to be fully committed to you and what you want.

You want hunger relieved, don't you, Lord?
You want resources to be shared out properly, right?
You want people like me to be willing to serve others,
I know that's what you want.

I think I would be of help
if I wanted what you want
Help me, Lord.

Dear Lord, We do thank you for all the food that we have on our tables each day. Please help those who live in countries that do not have food or clothing or houses to live in. Sometimes, because of our greed, we do not want to help those who are less fortunate than ourselves. Forgive us Lord, and help us to be generous in our giving.

We ask this in your Name, Amen.

The world is so big, God, and I'm so small and yet you care for me. Some days I see lots of people in the street and they look lonely and I wonder if they know that you love them and care for them too. Jesus can only help if we trust him. I pray for people who don't know Jesus. I pray they will start to look at the world around and realise how much nature shows your care. The rain and sun to make the plants grow. Fruit for us to eat. The sea for us to fish from. And behind all that, your fantastic care shown in sending Jesus to die for each one of us.

Help me to care enough about other people to let them know how much you care for them.

In Jesus' Name, Amen.

25 Morning and Evening

Glory to you my God
  this night 52

Psalm 4
Job chapter 11 verses 7–19
John chapter 14 verses 23–27

Hushed was the
  evening hymn 85

1 Samuel chapter 3 verses 1–19

It's a happy day 118

2 Peter chapter 1 verses 3–8
Psalm 77
Psalm 1

Lord dismiss us with
  your blessing 155

Isaiah chapter 40 verses 28–31
John chapter 14 verses 1–26
Galatians chapter 5 verses 16–26

Lord of all
  hopefulness 157

Mark chapter 10 verses 13–16
Psalm 121
Romans chapter 8 verses 28–39
Luke chapter 8 verses 22–25

Morning has
  broken 166

Genesis chapter 1 verses 14–19
Hosea chapter 6 verses 6
John chapter 9 verses 4–5

New every morning is
  the love 171

Lamentations chapter 3 verses
  22–26
Psalm 3
Psalm 5

Now the day is
  over 173

Psalm 139 verses 1–12
Psalm 121

Praise Him, praise
  Him, praise Him in
  the morning 202

Psalm 92 verses 1–5
Daniel chapter 6 verses 1–24
Psalm 113

Thank you Lord for
  this fine day 232

Psalm 33
Psalm 96
Psalm 103

The day you gave us Lord is ended   236

Psalm 121
Psalm 139

This is the day   255

Psalm 118
Genesis chapter 1 verses 1–8
Acts chapter 2
Matthew chapter 28 verses 1–9

When morning gilds the skies   278

Psalm 19
Psalm 5

Lord, we ask now to receive your blessing   301

Numbers chapter 6 verses 24–26
1 Corinthians chapter 13 verses 1–8
John chapter 17 verses 11–13

Prayers for Morning and Evening

Dear Lord, Right at the beginning of this day we want to take time to praise you for your greatness and for your goodness to us. Thank you for this day that you have given to us, for the people we will meet today, the food we will eat, the different things we will be able to do. Thank you Father for giving us life, help us to enjoy it to the full today.

In your Name, Amen.

Lord Jesus, Please help us today to live our lives for you. We want to please you today in the things we do and say, but we need your help. Thank you for your life within us that will give us the power to live as you want us to. Please fill our lives with yours today so that others will see you in us.

For your sake, Amen.

Heavenly Father, At the end of this day we want to come to you and ask you to forgive us for the bad things we have done today. We know there have been times that we have said things that have hurt others, or had unkind thoughts about people. Help us to put right whatever we can before the day ends.

Amen.

Lord, There's a saying, 'Today is the first day of the rest of your life'. That's a good way of looking at things, because I don't relly want to carry on in the way I've been going. I feel as though I need a fresh start to my life today, just like each morning brings a fresh start to the world. Could you make a difference in my life today Lord? Could you be like the sun coming up in the morning to bring light and warmth into my life? I really believe you can if I let you.

Thank you Lord, Amen.

O Lord, Yesterday was such a bad day and I can't see any reason why today should be any better. Except, that I'm starting today by asking for your help. You say that you've got a reason for me to live today, Lord. You've got a purpose for my life. Help me to find it today in some way. Show me something I can do today that will give today a value, even if it's just spending time with you, sharing my thoughts with you and letting you share yours with me. Please help me God.

Amen.

Lord, It seems that at the beginning of every day I have a decision to make. I'm either going to live today for myself and ignore you, or I'm going to do the things that you want and keep away from whatever's wrong.

When I've talking to you like this I know that I want to live today for you, but it'll probably be different later on when I'm with all my friends. Lord help me to remember that you will be with me all through the day, not just now, so all I have to do when I get tempted to do wrong is to pray quickly and ask you to help me right then. You will hear me when I call out to you won't you Lord?, because I know I'll need your help often.

Thank you Lord. Amen.

Lord, I started off today wanting to be good and I've blown it. I really didn't mean to do anything so bad, to hurt people, to make them cry. It was just the way things happened. I forgot to put others first, and tried to make everything work out the way I wanted it to. I'm sorry Lord, I really am. I'd like to be less selfish, more like you. Would you make me like that Lord? Change me, remake me.

Thank you Lord, Amen.

Heavenly Father, Some mornings the grass is covered with dew heavy and wet and there is mist lying above the ground. And then, only a few hours later, it's gone.

It's like me Lord – I start the day with so many good intentions and then halfway through the morning, I've forgotten them all. Is there something you could do about it Lord? Some strength you could put within me to help me do the things I intend to do? It'll need to come from *you* Lord, because I know I just don't have what it takes. Put your life in me Lord, live your life through me today.

Amen.

There's something special about the morning Lord. Early on, before everything gets going, it's so quiet and peaceful and still. Just how the world was when you first created it. The world seems to have lost that peace now. So much business and conflict and noise. Is it possible to know your peace even in the middle of all this, Lord? It's something I'd like to hold on to all through the day. Please fill my heart with peace. Thank you Lord.

Amen.

Lord God, Each day is new and different: we can never bring back yesterday – it's gone forever. That's why it's so important that we make the most of every day. We can only ever do that when we are walking in your ways and allowing you to show us what you want us to do. Please help us to live today trusting in you and your goodness to us.

In Jesus' Name, Amen.

Dear Heavenly Father, You know all the things that we are going to be doing today. Thank you for all the things we are going to enjoy, and thank you that you will be with us in the things that we find difficult. Thank you for your love for us today.

In Jesus' Name, Amen.

Thank you Lord God that we can meet together this morning to talk to you and sing about you. Please help us to think about you all through the day, to remember that you are always with us whatever we are doing and wherever we are.

Thank you that even when we go to bed at night you are with us looking after us while we are asleep.

In Jesus' Name, Amen.

Dear Lord Jesus, Sometimes we are afraid of the night-time and of the dark, and sometimes when we can't get to sleep at night we feel lonely and frightened. Thank you that we don't need to be afraid because you are always with us in the day and at night-time and you never go to sleep even when everyone else has. Please help us when we get frightened to remember to talk to you and know that you are with us.

In Jesus' Name, Amen.

Thank you Father for the gift of sleep: we know that we can only really enjoy what we do each day because we have time at night to rest and be refreshed. Thank you for providing everything that our bodies need to help them to work properly, so that we can enjoy healthy lives.

In Jesus' Name, Amen.

Lord, I'm dead beat,
shattered, pooped, absolutely crankimated!

I could've taken the day off,
left it all to somebody else,
and I do know I'm not indispensable,
but I did it all myself, Lord,
and I'm tired out.

Mind you,
I'm not complaining
It's a nice sort of feeling
a pleasant, job-well-done sort of weariness.

Thank you for giving us sleep.
Refresh me, Lord.

Lord Jesus, It's such a special feeling to come to the end of the day and know that you have been with me all through it. I feel so special to know that I'm your friend, so privileged to know that you were looking after me today. Thank you Lord for this warmth inside me, this excitement of knowing that you love me. I'm glad you'll be with me again tomorrow Lord – it makes each day something to look forward to Lord.

Thank you, Amen.

26   Praise and Thanksgiving

Abba Father   2

Romans chapter 8 verses 14–77
Mark chapter 14 verses 32–42
Matthew chapter 6 verses 5–15
Genesis chapter 11 verses 28,
   chapter 12 verse 9
Genesis chapter 22 verses 1–17

Alleluia, alleluia, give
   thanks to the risen
   Lord   3

Romans chapter 6 verses 3–10
Matthew chapter 28 verses 1–10

All people that on earth
   do dwell   4

Psalm 100
Psalm 149 verses 1–9

All things bright and
   beautiful   6

Genesis chapters 1–2 verse 3
Psalm 19
Psalm 65
Psalm 104
Psalm 148

Amazing grace! How
   sweet the sound   8

2 Corinthians chapter 12 verses
   8–10
Psalm 84 verses 1–12
Hebrews chapter 2 verses 8–18

At the name of
   Jesus   13

Philippians chapter 2 verses 5–11
Colossians chapter 1 verses 9–22
Acts chapter 1 verses 1–11
Ephesians chapter 1 verse 15,
   chapter 2 verse 10

Bless the Lord, O my
   soul   19

Psalm 103
Revelation chapter 19 verses 1–9
Mark chapter 11 verses 1–11

Blessed assurance   20

1 John chapter 1 verse 5, chapter
   2 verse 2
Colossians chapter 3 verses 1–17
John chapter 3 verses 1–17

Christ triumphant   25

John chapter 1 verses 1–14
Isaiah 52 verses 1–12
Hebrews chapter 10 verses 1–23
Revelation chapter 4 verses 1–11

Clap your hands all
you people   26

Psalm 149
Psalm 81

Come let us sing of a
wonderful love   29

John chapter 3 verses 1–21
1 John chapter 3 verses 16–24
John chapter 8 verses 1–11

Come and praise the
Lord our King   34

Luke chapter 2 verses 8–14
Ephesians chapter 1 verse 15,
chapter 2 verse 10
John chapter 14 verses 1–19

Dear Lord and Father
of mankind   37

Romans chapter 12 verses 1–8
Matthew chapter 4 verses 18–22
Genesis chapter 27 verses 1–46

Father, we adore
you   44

Psalm 95
John chapter 14 verses 21–26
John chapter 12 verses 1–8
Daniel chapter 3 verses 1–28
Acts chapter 6 verses 9–15,
chapter 8 verses 1–54

Father, we love
you   45

John chapter 12 verses 23–32
Psalm 86 verses 1–12
John chapter 16 verses 7–16

For the beauty of the
earth   48

Genesis chapter 1 verses 1–31
2 Peter chapter 1 verses 3–9
Psalm 8

From the rising of the
sun   49

Psalm 113
Psalm 148
Psalm 34
Acts chapter 3 verses 1–11

God is so good 53	Psalm 116 John chapter 8 verses 31–36 Luke chapter 8 verses 26–39
God is good 55	Psalm 100 verses 1–5 Hebrews chapter 4 verses 14–16 Psalm 34 verses 1–10

God is working His
  purpose out   57
	Isaiah chapter 11 verses 1–10
	Isaiah chapter 55 verses 6–11
	1 Thessalonians chapter 4 verse 13
	  to chapter 5 verse 11
	Jonah (extracts)

God who made the earth 63	Genesis 1 verses 1–31 2 Peter chapter 1 verses 3–9

Great is your
  faithfulness   64
	Psalm 65
	Lamentations chapter 3 verses
	  22–26
	Genesis chapter 8 verse 20,
	  chapter 9 verse 17
	Exodus chapter 16 verses 1–36,
	  chapter 17 verses 1–7

Hallelujah, for the Lord our God 66	Revelation chapter 19 verses 4–7 Psalm 9 verses 7–11 Daniel chapter 3 verses 1–28 1 Kings chapter 18 verses 17–40
Hallelu, Hallelu 67	Revelation chapter 19 verses 1–6 Psalm 138

Happiness is to
  know   70
	2 Corinthians chapter 5 verses
	  11–21
	Luke chapter 5 verses 16–26
	Psalm 16

He is Lord 75	Acts chapter 2 verses 34–36 Philippians chapter 2 verses 5–11 1 Corinthians chapter 15 verses 25–27 Revelation chapter 19 verses 1–9

He's got the whole world in His hands   78

Psalm 24
Genesis chapter 8 verse 21, chapter 9 verse 17
Deuteronomy chapter 33 verses 26–29

He's great, He's God   79

Colossians chapter 1 verses 9–19
Luke chapter 1 verses 30–33, 46–55
John chapter 14 verses 1–6

How great is our God   82

Exodus chapter 15 verses 1–8
Psalm 139 verses 7–10
Isaiah chapter 13 verses 15–19

How lovely on the mountains   84

Isaiah chapter 52 verses 7–10
Revelation chapter 19 verses 4–7
Isaiah chapter 54 verses 1–14
Matthew chapter 28 verses 16–20

I am so glad that my Father in heaven   88

John chapter 15 verses 9–17
Luke chapter 15 verses 1–7
John chapter 14 verses 16–26

I can run through a troop   90

Psalm 18 verses 1–3, 25–33
Psalm 62
Romans chapter 7 verse 14, chapter 8 verse 4

I'll be still   93

Psalm 46
John chapter 12 verses 1–11
Matthew chapter 6 verses 25–34
Luke chapter 10 verses 38–42

I'm very glad of God   107

Colossians chapter 1 verses 15–20
Psalm 95 verses 1–8

In my need Jesus found me   109

John chapter 10 verses 1–18
Luke chapter 15 verses 3–7

In the name of Jesus   111

Luke chapter 4 verses 1–13
1 John chapter 5 verses 1–5
Matthew chapter 8 verses 28–34

In the stars His handiwork I see 112	Psalm 19 Job chapter 38 verses 1–11, 22–29, chapter 42 verses 1–6 John chapter 10 verses 11–14, 27–30
I serve a risen Saviour 113	Matthew 28 verses 1–9 John chapter 11 verses 1–27 Romans chapter 5 verses 1–10 Hebrews chapter 5 verses 5a–8
It is a thing most wonderful 117	Romans chapter 5 verses 1–11 John chapter 3 verses 14–18 John chapter 14 verses 15–21
I've got peace like a river 120	John chapter 14 verses 23–27 Colossians chapter 3 verses 12–17 Galatians chapter 5 verses 16–26
I've got that joy, joy, joy, joy 121	Psalm 16 Isaiah 35 verses 1–10 John chapter 15 verses 1–17
I was lost but Jesus found me 125	Luke chapter 15 verses 3–7 Luke chapter 15 verses 8–10 Luke chapter 15 verses 11–32
I will sing, I will sing 126	Psalm 57 verses 7–11 Psalm 95 verses 1–7
I will sing the wondrous story 127	Luke chapter 15 verses 1–7 John chapter 5 verses 19–30 John chapter 20 verses 24–31
Jesus Christ is alive today 129	1 Corinthians chapter 15 verses 12–26 Colossians chapter 1 verses 9–19 Ephesians chapter 3 verses 14–19
Jesus, how lovely you are 133	Revelation chapter 22 verses 1–17 Luke chapter 24 verses 1–12 Revelation chapter 19 verses 1–9

Jesus is lord! 137   Colossians chapter 1 verses 9–20
                               Romans chapter 1 verses 18–20
                               Psalm 19

Jesus' love is very   John chapter 15 verses 9–17
  wonderful 139   1 John chapter 4 verses 7–10
                               Ephesians chapter 3 verses 14–21
                               Luke chapter 15 verses 11–32

Jesus loves me! 140   John chapter 3 verses 1–17
                               Mark chapter 10 verses 13–16
                               John chapter 14 verses 1–6
                               Luke chapter 8 verses 41–56

Jesus, Name above all   Philippians chapter 2 verses 5–11
  names 141   Isaiah chapter 9 verses 2, 6–7
                               Acts chapter 3 verses 1–16
                               Ephesians chapter 1 verses 15–23

Jubilate   Psalm 47
  everybody 145   Psalm 100
                               Colossians chapter 3 verses 12–17
                               Lamentations chapter 3 verses
                                 22–26

King of King and Lord   Revelation chapter 4 verses 1–11
  of Lords 148   Mark chapter 1 verses 1–11
                               Luke chapter 1 verses 26–33

Let's talk about   John 14 verses 1–6
  Jesus 150   John chapter 10 verses 1–9
                               Ephesians chapter 1 verses 15–23

Led like a lamb 151   Luke chapter 22 verses 22–65
                               Luke chapter 22 verse 66, chapter
                                 23 verse 25
                               Matthew chapter 28 verses 1–10
                               Luke chapter 24 verses 13–32

Let us praise God   John chapter 17 verses 1–5
  together 152   2 Timothy chapter 1 verses 1–10

Let us with a gladsome mind   154

Psalm 104
Psalm 118
Genesis chapter 1 verses 1–27

Lord Jesus Christ   156

1 John chapter 1 verse 5, chapter 2 verse 5
Matthew chapter 6 verse 1–18
1 Corinthians chapter 11 verses 23–32
Romans chapter 12 verses 1–21

Lord of all hopefulness   157

Mark chapter 10 verses 13–16
Psalm 121
Romans chapter 8 verses 28–39
Luke chapter 8 verses 22–25

Majesty   160

Philippians chapter 2 verses 5–11
Acts chapter 2 verses 14, 22–36
Revelation chapter 1 verses 9–18
Revelations chapter 4 verses 1–11

My faith is like a staff   168

Hebrews chapter 10 verse 38, chapter 11 verse 6
Luke chapter 7 verses 1–10
Ephesians chapter 6 verses 10–20

My God is so big   169

Luke chapter 1 verse 37
Romans chapter 8 verses 28–39
Exodus chapter 14 verses 13–31
Luke chapter 8 verses 22–25

My lord is higher   170

Psalm 18 verses 1–6, 16–36
Mark chapter 6 verse 45–52
Job chapter 38 verses 1–41

New every morning is the love   171

Lamentations chapter 3 verses 22–26
Psalm 3
Psalm 5

Now thank we all our God 175	Psalm 95 verses 1–7 Colossians chapter 1 verses 15–20 Luke chapter 17 verses 11–19
O Lord my God 179	Psalm 8 Romans chapter 5 verses 9–11 1 Thessalonians chapter 4 verses 16–17 John chapter 3 verses 16–18
Oh, oh, oh how good is the Lord 180	Acts chapter 3 verses 1–16 Ephesians chapter 1 verses 3–14 Psalm 103
One day when heaven was filled with His praises 187	Isaiah chapter 53 verses 1–9 Matthew chapter 27 verses 32–56 Luke chapter 24 verses 1–12
Our eyes have seen the glory 191	Acts chapter 1 verses 1–11 Ephesians chapter 1 verses 15–23
Praise Him on the trumpet 200	Psalm 150 Psalm 145
Praise Him, praise Him, all you little children 201	Luke chapter 24 verses 1–49 Psalm 61 Mark chapter 10 verses 13–16
Praise Him, praise Him, praise Him in the morning 202	Psalm 92 verses 1–5 Daniel chapter 6 verses 1–24 Psalm 113
Praise Him! praise Him! Jesus, our blessed redeemer 203	Luke chapter 24 verses 26–46 Psalm 61 Mark chapter 10 verses 13–16
Praise my soul 204	Revelation chapter 4 verses 1–11 Hebrews chapter 2 verses 9–18 Luke chapter 5 verses 16–26

Praise to the Lord our God 205	Psalm 47 Psalm 34 verses 1–10 Ephesians chapter 5 verses 1, 15–21
Rejoice in the Lord always 208	Philippians chapter 4 verses 4–9 Psalm 33 Psalm 63 1 Peter chapter 1 verses 3–8
Sing we the King 218	John chapter 1 verses 14–34 Psalm 24 Isaiah chapter 11 verses 1–10
Stand up and bless the Lord 224	Nehemiah chapter 9 verses 5b, 17, 31 Psalm 111 verses 1–10 Luke chapter 15 verses 11–32
Stand up, clap hands 225	Psalm 150 Acts chapter 3 verses 1–11 Psalm 23
Stand up, stand up for Jesus 226	Ephesians chapter 6 verses 10–20 2 Timothy chapter 2 verses 1–10 1 Corinthians chapter 9 verses 24–27 Romans chapter 8 verses 35–39
Tell me the old, old story 227	John chapter 3 verses 16–21 Colossians chapter 1 verses 9–23 Ephesians chapter 1 verses 3–14
Tell me the stories of Jesus 228	Luke chapter 10 verses 25–37 Luke chapter 15 verses 11–32 Matthew chapter 26 verses 36–46 Mark chapter 10 verses 13–16 Matthew chapter 28 verses 1–10
Tell out my soul 229	Mark chapter 5 verses 1–20 John chapter 4 verses 1–42 Psalm 30

Thank you   230   Luke chapter 17 verses 11–19
                              Psalm 116
                              Psalm 113

Thank you, thank you,   John chapter 20 verses 19–29
   Jesus   231   Romans chapter 8 verses 28–39
                              Ephesians chapter 5 verses 18–21

Thank you Lord for   Psalm 33
   this fine day   232   Psalm 96
                              Psalm 103

Thank you God for   John chapter 14 verses 23–27
   sending Jesus   233   1 Peter chapter 1 verses 13–21
                              John chapter 16 verses 5–15

Thank you Jesus   235   John chapter 3 verses 16–21
                              1 John chapter 3 verses 16–24
                              John chapter 20 verses 1–18
                              Matthew chapter 24 verses 29–51

The greatest thing in all   Philippians chapter 1 verses 21–30
   my life   239   Luke chapter 2 verses 41–52
                              1 Corinthians chapter 9 verses
                                 19–23

The joy of the Lord is   Acts chapter 3 verses 1–8
   my strength   240   Philippians chapter 4 verses 4–9
                              Nehemiah chapter 8 verses 1–12

The King of love   241   Psalm 23
                              John chapter 10 verses 1–21
                              Luke chapter 15 verses 1–7

The Lord's my   As For 241
   shepherd   243

The Lord is my   As for 241
   shepherd   244

There's a song of   Revelation chapter 19 verses 1–16
   exaltation   247   Revelation chapter 4 verses 1–11
                              Psalm 19

There's a new life in Jesus 249

1 John chapter 5 verses 1, 9–13
Psalm 32
Matthew chapter 9 verses 18–26

The steadfast love of the Lord 250

Lamentations chapter 3 verses 22–24
Romans chapter 8 verses 35–39
Genesis chapter 18 verses 17–23

This is the day 255

Psalm 118
Genesis chapter 1 verses 1–8
Acts chapter 2
Matthew chapter 28 verses 1–9

To God be the glory 259

John chapter 3 verses 1–17
John chapter 14 verses 1–14
Romans chapter 8 verses 1–11
Luke chapter 5 verses 16–26

We love to praise you, Jesus 265

John chapter 15 verses 1–17
John chapter 10 verses 1–18
Luke chapter 13 verses 22–30

We have heard a joyful sound 266

Luke chapter 19 verses 1–10
Acts chapter 4 verses 5–12
Isaiah chapter 45 verses 18–25
1 Timothy chapter 2 verses 1–5

We really want to thank you Lord 268

1 Corinthians chapter 12 verses 12–27
Ephesians chapter 4 verses 4–16

We've a story to tell to the nations 272

Isaiah chapter 59 verse 1, chapter 60 verse 3
Psalm 33
Isaiah chapter 2 verses 1–5

What a friend we have in Jesus 273

Matthew chapter 6 verses 25–34
John chapter 15 verses 1–17
Luke chapter 11 verses 1–13
Psalm 62

What a wonderful
  Saviour is
  Jesus   274

Philippians chapter 2 verses 1–11
1 Thessalonians chapter 4 verses
   13–18

When I survey the
  wondrous
  cross   277

Psalm 22
Matthew chapter 27 verses 27–50
Luke chapter 23

When morning gilds
  the skies   278

Psalm 19
Psalm 5

Wherever I am I'll
  praise Him   282

Psalm 34 verses 1–10
Psalm 63
Acts chapter 3 verses 1–11

Wherever I am I will
  praise you
  Lord   283

Psalm 40 verses 1–5
Acts chapter 3 verses 1–11
John chapter 7 verses 33–39

Will your anchor
  hold?   290

Psalm 62
Matthew chapter 8 verses 23–27
Mark chapter 6 verses 45–52

Yes, God is good   293

Psalm 65
Psalm 19
Ephesians chapter 1 verses 3–14

Yesterday, today,
  forever   294

Hebrews chapter 13 verses 1–9
Hebrews chapter 1 verses 1–12
2 Peter chapter 3 verses 1–12
Colossians chapter 2 verses 4–10

Your ways are
  higher   295

John chapter 14 verses 1–6
Isaiah chapter 55 verses 1–13
Romans chapter 11 verses 33–36

You are the king of
  glory   296

Isaiah chapter 9 verses 1, 6–7
Revelation chapter 4 verses 1–11
Hebrews chapter 1 verses 1–12
John chapter 6 verses 61–68

Yours be the glory 299	Matthew chapter 28 verses 1–10
	1 Corinthians chapter 15 verses 1–20
	Romans chapter 5 verses 1–11

Prayers of Praise and Thanksgiving

Heavenly Father, Thank you that you love us and fill our lives with good things. Thank you for the people who love us and care for us; for our families and friends, our teachers and all the others who help us to enjoy our lives.

Thank you that in this country we have so much to enjoy; so many toys to play with, houses that are warm and comfortable, clothes that we like wearing ans always enough food to eat. We pray for the people in other countries who do not have so many good things, and ask that you will show us how we can help them by sharing what we have.

In Jesus' Name, Amen.

Sometimes, Lord, There are things we don't feel very happy about and we don't feel like praising you for. But thank you that we can always praise you for who you are. We'll all just take a moment to say thank you to you for something about you that we *really* are thankful for. . . .

We know we'll all have thought of something different, because you made us all different. We thank you for that too.

In Jesus' Name, Amen.

Dear God, The psalms tell us to be joyful and glad because of what you have done for us. We are grateful to you because of your love for us: because you sent Jesus to forgive us when we deserved to be punished for what we have done wrong. Thank you for forgiving us instead of punishing us, thank you for loving us even though we do so much that is wrong. We are glad today because of you, and we thank you.

In Jesus' Name, Amen.

Dear God, Lots of people tell us that they love us: our Mummies and Daddies, grans and grandads, our best friends. We know that they mean it when they do something for us that is hard for them to do: my mummy cooks all my meals, washes, and irons all my clothes, daddy goes to work each day so that we have enough money. Thank you that you showed your love in the greatest way possible: you died for us so that we could be forgiven and become your children.

Thank you, God, Amen.

Dear God,
It's as if my eyes can see only good things;
as if life is suddenly keeping all its promises;
as if evil has been obliterated.
Oh yes,
I know it hasn't,
that I'll probably come down to earth with a dull
thump, that I might wake up in a minute with brainache,
but,
right now,
it's magic!

Life's a funny old mixture.

I know it can't always be like this,
but, for this experience of feeling great,
thank you, God.
It's fantastic!

Thank you Father that we can have such fun singing. Thank you for the gift of music and songs that we can enjoy. Help us to use the gifts that you have given us for your praise, so that as we sing songs together, you will know how much we love you. Thank you that knowing you and your love for us makes us want to sing beause we are happy.

In Jesus' Name, Amen.

Thank you Heavenly Father that we've so much to sing about; help us not to keep our song to ourselves. There are so many sad people in the world and even a lot of the songs people sing are sad. Thank you that in you we have real hope and joy and so we can sing from our hearts and not just our mouths. You put the song in the blackbird, you put the song of the wind in the trees and when I let you, you will put a song in me.

In Jesus' Name, Amen.

Dear God, Sometimes when we sing hymns and songs together it's easy to forget why we are singing and who we are singing to. Please teach us to sing our songs to you, to praise you because you are such a wonderful God and have done so much for us. We want to thank you for loving us and for making us your children. We know that because you are our Father you enjoy our singing and praise: we hope you will enjoy the songs we sing for you this morning.

In Jesus' Name, Amen.

I want to say
'Thank you, God!'
Thanks for being there,
thanks for listening,
thanks for having time for me,
thanks for all the good in the world:
good people, good things, good places;
if I can help at all,
with some of the not-so-good things,
here I am Lord –
grateful.

Sometimes, Lord, it's very hard to say 'thank you'. People do things for us everyday. Care for us. Cook for us. Teach us. Pray for us. Spend time with us. But we take it for granted and we don't say 'thank you'. It's the same with you, Lord. Today you made the sun come up. You gave us something to eat. You gave us friends. Above all, you gave us yourself. Help us to stop and take time to realise who you are and what you are doing. Soften our hearts so we can *really* thank you.

In your Name, Amen.

Father, Thank you for sending your son Jesus to save us. We have so much to praise and thank you for, but sometimes we forget what you did then and what you do now for us.

Help us to remember the gift of salvation and the promise of eternal life Father, once we remember these things we can't help but want to praise you.

In your precious Name, Amen.

Dear God, There are many things each day, to praise and thank you for – the way that you bring the sun up each morning, the way that you make the sunset each evening. We thank you that your love towards us is fresh every morning. Forgive us Lord because our love towards you is often stale and is like the morning dew that's here when the day starts but seems to disappear when the day progresses. Help us Lord to love you every minute of every day.

Amen.

Thank you Lord God, that in every country throughout the world there are people who love you and live their lives for you. Lord, we want your Name to be glorified in all the world through those who love you, so that many more people will turn to you and put their trust in you.

We ask it for your glory. Amen.

Lord Jesus, We want to praise and worship you today, not only in this time of singing, but throughout the day as we live our lives for you. Please accept our praise and fill us with your Holy Spirit that our lives might be pleasing to you today,

In your Name, Amen.

27   Prayers and Praying

Abba Father   2

Romans chapter 8 verses 14–17
Mark chapter 14 verses 32–42
Matthew chapter 6 verses 5–15
Genesis chapter 11 verses 28 to chapter 12 verse 9
Genesis chapter 22 verses 1–17

Ask! Ask! Ask! and it shall be given you   11

Luke chapter 11 verses 5–13
Luke chapter 12 verses 22–34
Matthew chapter 7 verses 7–14

Cleanse me from my sin, Lord   27

2 Kings chapter 5 verses 1–14
Psalm 51
Mark chapter 1 verses 40–45

Daniel was a man of prayer   36

Daniel chapter 6 verses 1–24

Father hear the prayer we offer   41

Luke chapter 22 verses 39–46
Mark chapter 1 verses 35–39
Genesis chapter 39 verses 1–23
Daniel chapter 6 verses 1–24

Father I place into your hands   42

Psalm 25
Psalm 139
Deuteronomy chapter 33 verses 26–29
Matthew chapter 6 verses 25–34

Father, lead me day by day   43

Luke chapter 4 verses 1–14
Mark chapter 1 verses 9–13
Exodus chapter 14 verses 1–31

Our Father who is in heaven   152

Matthew chapter 6 verses 9–15
Luke chapter 11 verses 1–13

Peter and John went to pray   198

Acts chapter 3 verses 1–11

Spirit of the living
  God   222

Acts chapter 2
Acts chapter 19 verses 1–6
John chapter 14 verses 15–26

Thank you God for
  sending Jesus   233

John chapter 14 verses 23–27
1 Peter chapter 1 verses 13–21
John chapter 16 verses 5–15

What a friend we have
  in Jesus   273

Matthew chapter 6 verses 25–34
John chapter 15 verses 1–17
Luke chapter 11 verses 1–13
Psalm 62

Teach us to Pray

Lord, Thank you that we don't ever need to feel hopeless about any situation because however bad things are we can always come and talk to you about it. Thank you for the way praying really does help. It seems to put things in perspective, reminds us that you are in control and gives us hope for the future. It's funny but often when we pray it seems to be us and our attitudes that you change, not our situation. That's quite a miracle!

Thank you Lord, Amen.

Heavenly Father, you tell us to love all men, but do you know how difficult that is? Well, yes, of course you do. But I'm not you, Lord, and there are some people I think I'll never abe able to love. Teach me to pray for these people that as I pray, your love for them will find a place in my heart. Sometimes maybe my prayers will mean that they change and become more lovable, but if not, that at least I'll be different.

Thank you Lord, Amen.

Is it true that you can hear every one of us when we pray Lord? So many people all speaking at once, all asking for different things? You must be bigger than all of us put together to do that. Wow! What a great God you are.

Praise you, Lord. Amen.

You always answer our prayers Lord. Sometimes you say 'yes' to what we ask, sometimes you say 'no' and sometimes you say 'wait'. Help me to accept whatever answer you give me.

> Amen.

Lord, your disciples came to you one day and asked you to teach them to pray. I'd like to learn more about praying. Sometimes I don't know what to say to you or how to pray for my friends and some days I find it hard to pray at all.

Thank you that your Holy Spirit living in us helps us to pray and shows us what we should be asking for. Please teach me more.

> In Jesus' Name, Amen.

Heavenly Father, When we pray you know just what's going on in our hearts. It's no good us saying things with our mouths when inside we have all kinds of wrong thoughts and bad attitudes. You'd rather we came to you and confessed our sins and asked you to make us clean, than pretend that there was nothing wrong in our lives. Please teach us to be honest with you so that you will hear our prayers and answer them.

> Thank you Lord, Amen.

Lord, Often when I pray I find it hard to believe that you will answer. You have promised us so many things and yet I don't always believe that you want to give those things to me. Lord, help me to know you better so that I can trust you to answer my prayers and fill my life in the way you have promised.

> Amen.

Dear God,
I heard my friend talking to you
just as if you're real,
just as if you're right here with us.
Now I'm talking to you.
I'm glad I can talk to you like this,
ordinary like, no fuss,
like chatting with a friend, or one of the family,
somebody I love.

It's more like a conversation,
which means, I suppose,
that, as well as talking to you I can listen,
just sit here, quiet,
and expect you to say something;
you speaking to me through my own throughts,
or someone else's words,
or the trees outside the window.
Help me to understand you,
please.

Dear God, Sometimes when I pray and ask you for something, you don't give it to me. Why not? I know that often
when I ask for something it is because I want it: maybe you
know that I don't really need it and that it's best not to give
it to me. Thank you for giving me everything I need: please
help me to know the difference between what I want and
what I need.

Amen.

I'm finding it hard to pray, God;
I never know what to say.
Well, all right, *sometimes* I don't know what to say.
I don't think I'm afraid of you,
or embarrassed by you,
or short of things to talk about;
I think it's because I'm just not used to praying.
Maybe, because, for me,
praying seems such an odd thing to do,
I'm tongue-tied.
Can you help me, please?

Thank you Lord Jesus that you are alive today and that you
want to look after us all. Thank you that we can talk to you
and know that you will listen to us. Please teach us how to
pray more; to talk to you as our best friend, knowing that as
we tell you our problems you will help us and will be with
us.

We pray in your Name, Amen.

Lord, so often we are so busy with our lives that we don't
spend enough time with you. Forgive us for this Lord, and

please teach us to be still before you, waiting upon you and knowing that you are our God. Please speak to us Lord.

Amen.

Heavenly Father, We thank you that you love to answer our prayers. We ask that you will teach us how to pray for the right things so that we don't become selfish in the things that we ask for. Teach us to pray for other people: those who are sick or lonely and for those who don't know you. We pray today especially for (insert names). Thank you for hearing our prayer.

In Jesus' Name, Amen.

28　Service and Giving

A boy gave to Jesus　1　Luke chapter 9 verses 10–17
Mark chapter 6 verses 30–44

Be bold　14　Exodus chapters 3 and 4
Joshua chapter 1 verses 6–9
Deuteronomy chapter 31 verses 1–8
1 John chapter 4 verses 11–18
1 Samuel chapter 17 verses 1–58

Father, I place into your hands　42　Psalm 25
Psalm 139
Deuteronomy chapter 33 verses 26–29
Matthew chapter 6 verses 25–34

Give me oil in my lamp　50　Matthew chapter 25 verses 1–13
Zachariah chapter 1 verses 1–14
John chapter 14 verses 15–26

God forgave my sin　54　Psalm 32
Matthew chapter 6 verses 9–15
Ephesians chapter 4 verses 17–32
Matthew chapter 10 verses 1–15
Luke chapter 21 verses 1–4

He gave me eyes so I could see　74　Psalm 139
John chapter 9 verses 1–34
Mark chapter 2 verses 1–12

I am a lighthouse　87　Matthew chapter 5 verses 13–16
Luke chapter 8 verses 22–25
Zachariah chapter 1 verses 1–14

If you see someone　95　Luke chapter 10 verses 30–37
Matthew chapter 25 verses 31–46

I sing a song of the saints　115　Psalm 145 verses 1–13
Hebrews chapters 11–12 verse 1
2 Corinthians chapter 6 verses 1–10

Jesus bids us shine 128	Luke chapter 11 verses 33–36 John chapter 1 verses 1–12 John chapter 8 verses 12 Isaiah chapter 59 verses 1–2, 8–10, chapter 60 verses 1–3
Jubilate, everybody 145	Psalm 47 Psalm 100 Colossians chapter 3 verses 12–17 Lamentations chapter 3 verses 22–26
Make me a channel of your peace 161	Psalm 37 verses 1–11 Matthew chapter 5 verses 1–16 2 Corinthians chapter 1 verses 2–7 Matthew chapter 6 verses 9–15 Mark chapter 8 verses 34–38
Make me a servant 162	Matthew chapter 20 verses 20–28 Luke chapter 22 verses 14–27 John chapter 13 verses 1–16 Acts chapter 20 verses 28–35
May the mind of Christ my Saviour 165	Philippians chapter 2 verses 1–11 Psalm 1 Psalm 119 verses 1–16 John chapter 14 verses 23–28
One more step along the world I go 188	Psalm 48 John chapter 10 verses 11–18, 27–30 Romans chapter 12 verses 1–2 Philippians chapter 4 verses 4–9
Peace I give to you 196	John chapter 14 verses 23–31 John chapter 7 verses 37–39 1 Corinthians chapter 13 verses 1–8
The greatest thing in all my life 239	Philippians chapter 1 verses 21–30 Luke chapter 2 verses 41–52 1 Corinthians chapter 9 verses 19–23

The Lord has need of   Matthew chapter 25 verses 14–30
   me   242   2 Timothy chapter 2 verses 1–10
                            2 Timothy chapter 4 verses 1–8
                            1 Samuel chapter 3 verses 1–19

There's new life in   1 John chapter 5 verses 1, 9–13
   Jesus   249   Psalm 32
                            Matthew chapter 9 verses 18–26
                            John chapter 11 verses 1–44

When I needed a   Matthew chapter 25 verses 31–46
   neighbour   275   Luke chapter 10 verses 30–37

Who is on the Lord's   Matthew chapter 12 verses 24–27
   side?   287   1 Samuel chapter 17 verses 1–51
                            Psalm 98
                            2 Timothy chapter 2 verses 1–10

Lord, we ask now to   Numbers chapter 6 verses 24–26
   receive your   1 Corinthians chapter 13 verses
   blessing   301   1–8
                            John chapter 17 verses 11–13

Prayers to do with Service and Giving

Lord, When I think of my future I often wonder what I'll do. There are so many choices Lord, lots of interesting careers and jobs. Most of all I'd like my future to involve serving you and serving other people in some way. There are a lot of people who need help and although my life doesn't seem very much, I'd like you to use me even in a small way.

Here I am Lord, please show me which way to go.

In Jesus' Name, Amen.

Lord, When we think of serving you with our lives, we usually think of going out to other people to help them in different ways. Although that's important, you also want us to take time to be with you. One of the greatest ways we can serve you is to bring you our thanks and praise and yet we often find that the hardest thing to do. We want our songs and prayers to be like gifts to you, to make you glad and to tell you how much we love you. Please accept our worship.

> In Jesus' Name, Amen.

Lord, We usually find it quite easy to help those around us who are our friends and people we know. But you showed in the story of the good Samaritan that we should be willing to help all those in need, even if they are strangers or people we don't like very much. Next time we have the opportunity, make us willing to do all we can to help someone like that.

> For your Sake, Amen.

Lord Jesus, You said that if we see someone in need in any way and help them, it's as though we have helped you personally. That's a real privilege Lord, and we ask that you will give us many opportunities to help others to show how we love you.

> In your Name, Amen.

Heavenly Father, In the Bible it says 'God loves a cheerful giver'. Forgive me that very often when I have to share or give something away I am resentful and cross instead of cheerful. Help me to be glad that I can do something for others and help me always to remember that what I have really belongs to you anyway, and is yours to give where you want.

> In Jesus' Name, Amen.

Lord, why does it sometimes seem such a struggle to do the things you want me to. It's not always easy being a Christian. You warned your disciples that unless they were prepared to give up their lives completely to you, there was no point starting out to follow you. Lord, when it seems hard to do the things you ask, please help me to keep going. Make me prepared to go the extra mile in helping others, not just to do as little as I can get away with. Help me to be a servant as you were.

> In your Name, Amen.

Lord Jesus, It's so much easier in life just to do the things that *I* enjoy and that make *me* happy. I find it hard to put other people first and think about what's best for them. But part of being a Christian is learning not to be selfish so I know I need to change. Lord Jesus, please help me to think of others as being more important than myself and to put their needs first. I know that's what you would do and I ask it in your Name.

Amen.

Heavenly Father, Someone once said 'A man is no fool who gives what he cannot keep, to gain what he cannot lose'. Teach us how to give our lives to you completely so that we might receive your gift of eternal life.

In Jesus' Name, Amen.

Lord Jesus, You said that it is wrong to boast about the times we help other people or the times we give away our money. You know how easy it can be to boast because we want others to think that we are good. Help us to be content to know that you have seen what we've done and that we will be rewarded for it in heaven if we keep quiet about it here on earth.

Teach us to be secret givers.

In your Name, Amen.

Dear God, Thank you for that lovely story in the Bible of how an old lady brought everything she had as a gift to the temple. Even though it was such a small amount it pleased you far more than the enormous gift from a man who was very rich and still kept lots for himself.

You know, Lord, that I don't have very much and often I want to keep what I have for myself. Please help me to be willing to give generously and share what I have with those who are in need. Teach me that it really is far better to give than to receive.

In Jesus' Name, Amen.

29 Times of Sadness

Amazing grace! How sweet the sound 8

2 Corinthians chapter 12 verses 8–10
Psalm 84 verses 1–12
Hebrews chapter 2 verses 8–18

Be still and know that I am God 22

Psalm 46
John chapter 14 verses 23–27
Luke chapter 8 verses 22–25
Luke chapter 10 verses 38–42

Father, hear the prayer we offer 41

Luke chapter 22 verses 39–46
Mark chapter 1 verses 35–39
Genesis chapter 39 verses 1–23
Daniel chapter 6 verses 1–24

Father, I place into your hands 42

Psalm 25
Psalm 139
Deuteronomy chapter 33 verses 26–29
Matthew chapter 6 verses 25–34

Great is your faithfulness 64

Psalm 65
Lamentations chapter 3 verses 22–26
Genesis chapter 8 verse 20, chapter 9 verse 17
Psalm 19
Exodus chapter 16 verses 1–36, chapter 17 verses 1–7

I am trusting you Lord Jesus 86

John chapter 14 verses 1–6, 15–21
Psalm 25
Proverbs chapter 3 verses 1–7
Luke chapter 8 verses 41–56

I do not know what lies ahead 92

Matthew chapter 6 verses 23–34
Psalm 48
Isaiah chapter 58 verses 8–14

I'll be still   93

Psalm 46
John chapter 12 verses 1–11

Jesus loves me!   147

John chapter 3 verses 1–17
Mark chapter 10 verses 13–16
John chapter 14 verses 1–6
Luke chapter 8 verses 41–56

Kumbaya   149

Ecclesiastes chapter 3 verses 1–11
Psalm 42
Luke chapter 10 verses 30–37
Psalm 147

Make me a channel of
  your peace   161

Psalm 37 verses 1–11
Matthew chapter 5 verses 1–16
2 Corinthians chapter 1 verses 2–7
Matthew chapter 6 verses 9–15
Mark chapter 8 verses 34–38

Now be strong and
  very
  courageous   122

Joshua chapter 1 verses 1–9
1 John chapter 4 verses 11–18
Psalm 27
Isaiah chapter 41 verses 1–5
Exodus chapters 3, 4

Shalom my friend   217

John chapter 14 verses 23–31
Psalm 29
Isaiah chapter 26 verses 3–12

The King of love my
  shepherd is   241

Psalm 23
John chapter 10 verses 1–21
Luke chapter 10 verses 1–7

The Lord's my
  shepherd   243

Psalm 23
John chapter 10 verses 1–21
Luke chapter 15 verses 1–7

The steadfast love of
  the Lord   250

Lamentations chapter 3 verses
  22–24
Romans chapter 8 verses 35–39
Genesis chapter 18 verses 17–23

Turn your eyes upon Jesus 260	Colossians chapter 3 verses 1–17 Luke chapter 9 verses 27–36 Revelation chapter 1 verses 9–18
What a friend we have in Jesus 273	Matthew chapter 6 verses 25–34 John chapter 15 verses 1–17 Luke chapter 11 verses 1–13 Psalm 62
Yesterday, today, forever 294	Hebrews chapter 13 verses 1–9 Hebrews chapter 1 verses 1–12 2 Peter chapter 3 verses 1–12 Colossians chapter 2 verses 4–10

Prayers in Times of Sadness

Lord, why? Why did you let that happen? Why didn't you stop the accident from happening? Why did people have to die? Are there any answers Lord? Are we ever going to understand· It's your world Lord; why don't you do something?

Lord Jesus, you cried once. You know what it's like to have a special friend die. You understand the way I feel, the loneliness, the emptiness, the awfulness of knowing I'll never be able to share my secrets with my friend again, to laugh together, cry together, grow up together. Lord, will anything ever stop this pain, fill this emptiness. Lord will you?

Lord, I didn't know it was possible to be so hurt by the people you thought loved you. It's taken me by surprise Lord, and left me feeling that no-one cares. You must have felt like this on the cross when everyone abandoned you and even your Father turned away from you. You had no-one then, but at least I have you. You're all I've got Lord, please be everything I need.

Amen.

Lord, I don't know if I can cope with what has happened. I feel as though I never want to meet people again. I even feel that it would be better to be dead. Lord, give me courage to face another day. Help me to trust you for the future Lord, and just get on with today. At least I know you love me and that love will never end.

Thank you Lord, Amen.

Lord, when one of our friends is sad and hurting, we all feel sad too. We want to be able to help, to show that we care. How can we do that today Lord? Make us sensitive to see what needs doing, what needs to be said. Make us willing to help in whatever way we can.

In Jesus' Name, Amen.

Lord, You can bring good from bad. You can change sorrow to joy. You can heal the brokenhearted. Your love, Lord, changes the worst situation. Bring something good from this time Lord, change these people's sorrow into joy. Heal those who are brokenhearted because of what has happened. Help them Lord, be close to them, give them your strength.

In Jesus' Name, Amen.

I don't think anyone can have felt like this before. What's happened to me Lord? My life has lost its meaning and I feel numb. I thought I would have cried, been sad, felt torn apart. But there's nothing like that Lord. Just this numbness, as though nothing will ever matter again. Do something, Lord, melt the ice that is slowly freezing my heart, soften the hardness that is turning me to stone. Bring me back to life Lord. Please.

Amen.

Lord, is it true that you know everything about us? Do you really see the tears I cry, the pain that I hold inside? Too embarrassed to let others know, I hide it away, pretend everything's all right. But you see; when everyone else has gone and I'm left with nothing else except this constant pain, you're there. Sometimes I feel that you want to touch me, to take away that pain, to heal those scars. Your gentleness overwhelms me and my tears become tears of joy; the joy of knowing that you care, you love, you are here.

30   Work and Play

Brothers and
  sisters   21

Galatians chapter 3 verse 26,
  chapter 4 verses 7
Ephesians chapter 4 verses 1–16
Psalm 133

Father I place into your
  hands   42

Psalm 25
Psalm 139
Deuteronomy chapter 33 verses
  26–29
Matthew chapter 6 verses 25–34

Father, lead me day by
  day   43

Luke chapter 4 verses 1–14
Mark chapter 1 verses 9–13
Exodus chapter 14 verses 1–31

In our work and in our
  play   108

Luke chapter 2 verses 41–52
Galatians chapter 5 verses 16–26
Mark chapter 10 verses 13–16

I sing a song of the
  saints   115

Psalm 145 verses 1–13
Hebrews chapters 11 verse 1 to
  chapter 12 verse 1
2 Corinthians chapter 6 verses
  1–10

It's a happy day   118

2 Peter chapter 1 verses 3–8
Psalm 77
Psalm 1

I want to live for Jesus
  every day   122

Luke chapter 12 verses 16–21
Luke chapter 18 verses 18–27
Mark chapter 8 verses 34–38

Just as I am, your child
  to be   146

Luke chapter 14 verses 15–24
Matthew chapter 11 verses 25–30
Luke chapter 15 verses 11–32
1 Samuel chapter 3 verses 1–19

Put your hand in the
  hand   206

Matthew chapter 8 verses 23–27
Luke chapter 5 verses 1–11
John chapter 2 verses 13–17

Though the world has forsaken God 257	Matthew chapter 7 verses 13–20 John chapter 13 verses 31–35 Acts chapter 2 verses 14–21, 41–47 Joshua chapter 2 verses 1–21
Wherever I am 282	Psalm 34 verses 1–10 Psalm 63 Acts chapter 3 verses 1–11
Wherever I am I will praise you Lord 283	Psalm 40 verses 1–5 Acts chapter 3 verses 1–11 John chapter 7 verses 33–39

Prayers for Work and Play

Heavenly Father, There are so many people without a job that it makes me think *I* may never get one. And then what will I do with all that time each day? It makes me quite worried sometimes. Help me use my time wisely now in studying so that I will get some qualifications and also in developing hobbies and interests that I can do in my spare time.

Thank you that I can trust you with my future and know that whatever happens, you will always have things for me to do. Thank you Lord.

In Jesus' Name, Amen.

Lord Jesus, At work there aren't many people who believe in you. It's sad because they are missing so much. Please use my life to speak to them by the way I do my work, by the way I talk and the way I care for others. Please give me opportunities to tell them about you and help me never to be ashamed of the fact that I belong to you.

In your Name, Amen.

Lord, I want to thank you that I have a job. I know there are many people who would love to be at work but can't find any. So even when it's a struggle to get up in the morning, remind me to be thankful that I've got a job to go to. And help me to do it as well as I can.

For your sake. Amen.

Lord, Sometimes I feel things at work are so unfair. The hours, the pay, the way we're treated. It makes me feel that I can't be bothered to work hard if that's all I get in return. I know that you helped me to get that job though, so I suppose in some ways I'm there for you. Help me to do my work for you and to forget about the others. Thank you that you will notice when I do my job well and you will be pleased. That makes me want to work harder.

Thank you Lord. Amen.

Lord, It's hard to work when I see lots of money around and know that no-one would really notice if I took some. You'd see though and I know it wouldn't be right. I just want to ask for your help so that if I'm tempted you'll give me the strength not to take it.

Thanks Lord, Amen.

Lord, Sometimes it's hard at work when all the others want to do is waste time and mess around. I know we've got to do the job and I feel that because I'm a Christian I should set an example. It's hard though, Lord, because they all just laugh. Please give me the courage to carry on doing what's right.

In your Name, Amen.

Heavenly Father, I just want to say thank you for all the games I can play with my friends. We have a great time and somehow I feel that you must be pleased to see us having such fun.

Thanks Lord, Amen.

Lord Jesus, I didn't realise that there could be games that are harmful. I thought everyone was just having a joke, and then it got pretty scary. Lord, help me to be wise about the games I get involved in and when I know something's wrong, help me keep away from it.

Thank you Lord, Amen.

Lord, We won, and I'm really proud! It was a great game and so close! The other team looked pretty disappointed at the end, so would I if we'd lost. Maybe it would be good to tell them how well they played to cheer them up. Help me to do that Lord.

Amen.

Father, Some of my friends get so rough when we play games. It starts off as fun, but then it gets silly and spoils it all. Please help us to care for one another when we are playing. Help me not to join in when I know I shouldn't. Even when I'm playing, I want people to see that I'm Christian by the way I behave.

Please help me Lord. Amen.

Lord, You know how hard it is not to be angry when someone else has won a game by cheating or when an unfair decision is made. I get mad inside and want to argue or fight with the other people and I feel that I never want to play with them again. I suppose that's not right as a Christian. You said we have to learn to forgive others. Well, please help me Lord, help me to control my feelings and make me willing to forgive.

In your Name, Amen.

Heavenly Father, I have so many toys and games to play with. Thank you for them all. Please help me to remember that you want me to share them with others so they can enjoy them as well.

In Jesus' Name, Amen.

Lord, sometimes when I'm playing a game, I want to win so much that I start to cheat. But then if I do win it's spoilt because I know it wasn't really fair. Help me to enjoy games even when I don't win, that just taking part will be fun. Next time I'm tempted to cheat, please stop me.

Thank you Lord, Amen.